# BLOOD RELATIVES

*A True Story*
*of Family Secrets and Murders*

by
Lori Carangelo

Access Press

Cover photos (Left to Right): Sandra Cano Sauceda aka Mary Doe in Doe v. Bolton (public access photo); Joel Lee Domingues Jr. (provided by Joel Lee with signed release); Melissa Fuss Able Erives; Charles Fuss; and Margaret Fuss Branch (Georgia Department of Corrections public access photos)

2

# CONTENTS

# Dedication

*In memory of the lives that could have been,
had there been no "family secrets."*

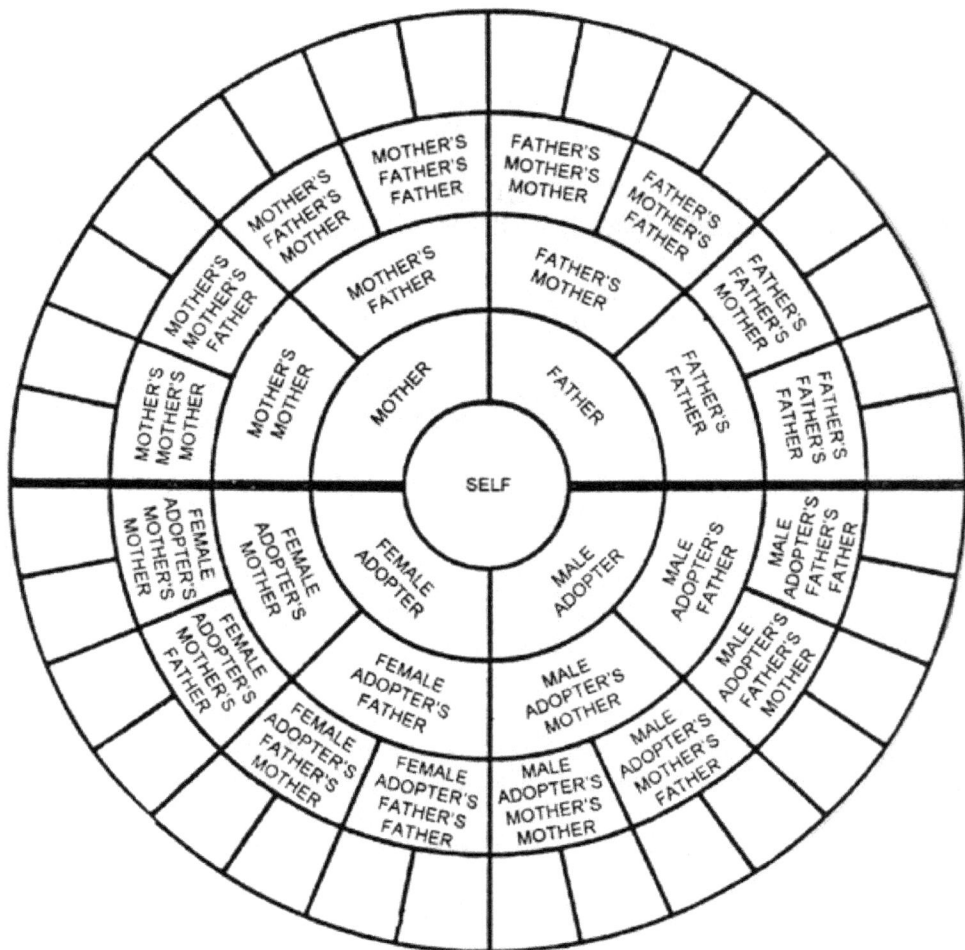

An Adoptee's Family Circle

> *"The human soul is difficult to interfere with–*
> *You hesitate how far you should go."*
> -Rev. Loring Charles Brace,
> who initiated the Orphan Trains.

## 1.
## CHARLES
### *AND THE BLOODY MURDER OF JACKIE FUSS*

To this day, many folks in Decatur, Georgia, still remember the murders. The first one was on June 21, 1996, officially the first day of summer, the summer solstice, and everyone was complaining that it was *"hot enough to fry an egg on the sidewalk."*

In the late afternoon, a woman phoned the Sheriff's office and reported seeing a tall, skinny man running down the road *"buck naked."* The anonymous caller volunteered that she recognized the streaker as being 31-year old Charles Fuss. Neither the caller's identity, nor why Charles was naked and running at the most sweltering time of day, was of any particular interest to the deputy who took the call. It was not the first time he had got a complaint about Charles. He was just glad to be on dispatch duty in front of a big old fan instead of chasing down the *"usual drunks and crazies"* that Friday night.

Sydney Dorsey, 56, a Homicide Detective, and Officer Melvin Walker, 32, happened to be in the area when they heard the dispatch about Charles. As they pulled up to the Fuss home, the sky was a blaze of red while the sun began its descent toward the horizon. Dorsey was annoyed at having to delay his dinner to go look for Charles, so, before rounding him up, he was going to give Jackie Fuss a good talking to about her boy. But even in the fading light the detective's instinct told him something *"wasn't right."* The front door was ajar and the old wood framed screen door was creaking back and forth on its rusted hinges from what the deputy called *"a sorry excuse for an evening breeze"* that didn't cool their sweaty brows.

5

"*Maybe she went out and forgot to lock up,*" Melvin suggested. But it wasn't like Jackie to leave a door open like that. This time of year, folks took care to keep out the gnats, flies and creepy crawlers. And everyone knew the reclusive rich widow was paranoid that someone might steal her hoard of antiques and collectibles. Dorsey called out, but not too loudly in order not to startle the elderly woman. "*Miz Fuss?... Jackie?*" No response. Then louder, "*JACK EEE?*" Again, no response.

As Dorsey cautiously led the way into the darkness, neither man noticed the blood smear inside the door jamb nor the broken ceramic lamp amid all the clutter on the living room floor. "*What the....?*" Dorsey muttered as he stumbled over unidentifiable junk. Upon reaching the dining room, both men suddenly stopped in their tracks. A dusty crystal chandelier sent the day's final prisms of light traveling down the faded parchment colored wallpaper to the rug. "*Hold it!*" warned Dorsey in a whisper as he put his finger to his lips, and then "*Shhhh,*" as he pointed to the red footprints on Jackie's prized Persian rug.

The men un-holstered their guns in unison as they cautiously approached the kitchen, instinctively expecting the worst, as a familiar odor of decomposing flesh reached their nostrils. But as Dorsey reached inside the kitchen and flipped on the light switch, nothing could have prepared them for what was on the other side of the door. What follows is the version that the local gossips would relish for some time to come.

"*JESUS MARY JOSEPH!!! OohhmyGAWD! OOOOhhhGAWD... myyyy GAWD !!* " Dorsey kept wailing. Melvin vomited.

According to the locals' version of what they later heard about the grisly scene, there lay Jackie Fuss, or *parts* of her, in a blackish-red slime of her own blood, one bloody arm over here, a bloody leg over there, her bloody neck slashed ear-to-ear so deeply that her head was

6

almost decapitated. Blood was everywhere at the gruesome scene - on the walls, cabinets - everything had been liberally spray-painted red with her blood. The 71-year old woman had been hacked to pieces on her own kitchen floor.

In the "official" version, however, Jackie was found in her basement, lifeless from a single blow to her head with an axe, somehow with very little blood splatter. In either version, the first axe blow that pierced her skull when her killer attacked her from behind would have resulted in instant death, which explained why no blood curdling scream was heard through the screens on her open windows. Whichever version is to be believed, the weapon, a full size bloody axe with a wood handle of about 36 inches, was still at the scene.

Dorsey muttered *"This is not good."* But he wasn't referring to Jackie's bad luck. Dorsey would be up for election as Sheriff in November, not a good time for a man aspiring to be the county's first Black Sheriff to be saddled with an unsolved axe murder of a prominent citizen on his watch. On the other hand, this could be the slam dunk Dorsey needed, since he was sure he could nail Charles as the perpetrator. Charles routinely used the axe (aka murder weapon) to chop wood for the fireplace in winter, so his fingerprints would surely be on the wood handle.

It was impossible to traverse the scene without compromising evidence, so for the time being, no one would be allowed to enter the home to retrieve what there was of poor Jackie, nor her possessions. Dorsey knew he was going to miss dinner that night, but it shouldn't take long to track down and arrest Charles as more callers reported seeing a *"naked man"* streak by their windows in the light of the full moon.

Screaming police sirens, revolving red lights, car doors slamming, the clamor of male voices shouting, and yellow crime scene tape told neighbors what the racket was about. Those who were questioned reported frequently hearing arguments between Jackie and her boy. Next morning, local media identified Charles as *"the only suspect"* in a *"rage killing"* of the woman whose late husband had been well known for his local philanthropy and who *"from the goodness of their hearts had adopted and raised the ungrateful boy."*  Although the first "official" news report said Jackie's body was discovered in Charles' basement bedroom, subsequent news stories added that he "lured" Jackie to the basement bedroom on the pretense of looking under the bed for a misplaced item, then whacked her while her back was turned to him. But most damning is that, after Charles was found miles away, he immediately *confessed* to the murder... *which he may not have committed.* The story of how Charles came to be part of Jackie's life, and the only suspect in her murder, then began to unfold.

It was an icy cold, dreary December day in 1965, when 20-year old Joyce Burge gave birth to Charles.  He was the third of the Burge children born in Cartersville, a small sleepy suburb 42 miles from bustling downtown Atlanta.  Joyce said she gave up both Charles and David for adoption because they could not afford all three children. But she would only allow the brothers to be adopted out *"on condition they not be separated."* As was the practice then, and still is, the relinquished boys' birth records were legally falsified, their adoptive parents named on their records as if they were the parents at time of their births, and the true birth certificates were sealed in the court once their adoptions were finalized.  All parties were then forever bound by secrecy under Georgia state law.

Inez Hyde Fuss, who everyone knew as "Jackie," was born in 1925 and lived all of her 71 years in Decatur, a suburb within Atlanta known as *"a city of homes, schools and places of worship."* There, she met and married William "Bill" Fuss, who was the same age, and they had a daughter, Margaret.  The Fuss family lived in a spacious home on Sue Lane, an upscale neighborhood where they had planned to have more children.  But try as they did, Margaret remained their only child until 1965, when Bill and Jackie began to consider adopting.

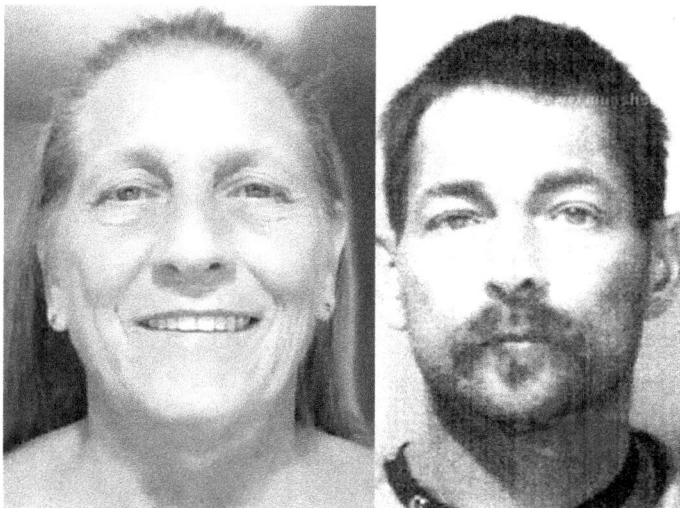

Joyce Burge
and her biological son, David Fuss
adopted by Bill and Jackie Fuss

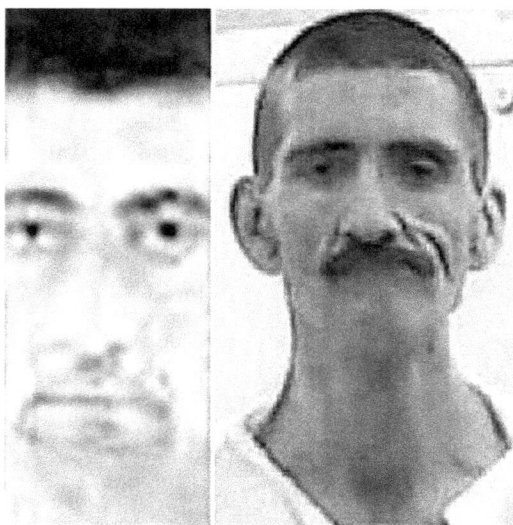

Charles Fuss, Joyce Burge's other biological son
also adopted by Bill and Jackie Fuss
(Before & After Prison)

Fertility treatments did not exist until the first "test tube baby" made headlines in 1978, so adoption was their only option. Bill was doing well in his business as a building contractor when they adopted both Charles and David.

Although Jackie and Bill had talked about also adopting a girl "to round out the family," it was apparent from the start that Jackie had already taken on more than she could handle with two demanding baby boys and their own equally demanding teenage girl.

But a few years later, when Bill heard about a beautiful baby girl with strawberry blonde hair who had escaped being aborted, Bill, a staunch Pro-Life Baptist, felt it was pre-ordained that they should rescue this child. Not to disappoint Bill, Jackie tried to show enthusiasm when they adopted Melissa in 1970.

The identity of Melissa's mother was supposed to be confidential to avoid publicity about the thwarted abortion and the adoption. But when the mother, her newborn clutched in her arms, was being discharged from the hospital, they were unceremoniously pushed in a wheelchair into an elevator where Jackie, Bill and Margaret were waiting. The mother's tears blurred the surreal scene as Bill Fuss handed her an envelope containing $200 cash as she reluctantly handed over Melissa to Jackie as instructed. *"Y'all take care of ma daughter"* was all the mother had a chance to say.

It was a done deal.

Unlike a lot of children adopted in the 1960s and 1970s whose adoptions were kept secret from them indefinitely, Charles, David and Melissa always knew they were adopted because Margaret, the oldest, had always known. But their biological parents' identities were a secret that only Jackie knew, from court papers in their safe deposit box, and she vowed never to disclose it.

There was obvious sibling rivalry from the start. Until the adoptions, Margaret had been the spoiled "only child," the "real" child of her "real" parents, as she saw it. Now, three young adoptive siblings needed Jackie's full attention. As the children grew, so did the problems.

At times, Margaret, even in her twenties and beyond, would assert "her place" in the family. If her younger siblings teased her, as siblings do, by calling her names such as *"Mama's Girl,"* and *"Ugly Duckling,"* Margaret had a ready retort: *"At least ma mamma didn't give me away like your mamma did!"* More often they all "joined forces" when all four children retaliated against Jackie who tried to keep them in line. So it was not uncommon for neighbors to hear loud arguments between Jackie and her brood, but never a peep out of Bill who learned to escape the melee by spending long hours building his lucrative contracting business.

It was also obvious to neighbors that Jackie was a verbally abusive mother. In fact, they referred to Jackie as *"one evil lady."*

Charles, at 28, was still single and still living at home with Jackie while the other Fuss children, then in their 30s, had already moved out after Bill finally worked himself to death, succumbing to a major heart attack.

David and Margaret escaped the fray by finding someone to marry - as did Melissa at 16.

But Charles, who couldn't seem hold a job long enough to leave the nest, remained a constant thorn in Jackie's rear end as she tried to keep a tight reign on her boy who some called "slow" and others called "crazy."

Perhaps a symptom of her grief after Bill's death, or more likely because she then had full control of Bill's estate, reportedly totaling *a million dollars*, Jackie's spending – and hoarding – was out of control. It was difficult to walk through the house without bumping into or stumbling over piles of newly acquired junk. Eventually, neither Charles nor Jackie could find a place to sit because the clutter completely hid the sofa.

Unable to cope with Charles' unpredictable "acting out" behaviors that ranged from "the silent treatment" to tantrums when ordered to do a chore, Jackie's verbal abuse increased over time.

In an attempt to get enough money to break free, Charles tried his hand at armed robbery.

Covering the lower half his face with a bandana for a half-ass disguise, and brandishing one of Bill's guns that had never been locked away, he took a deep breath and nervously made a bee-line for the man behind the cash register. But when the liquor store owner pointed his own gun at Charles, the unexpected stand-off proved too much for Charles... who promptly passed out. Police revived him and took him into custody.

After serving his time, Charles had nowhere else to go but home to Jackie who was never going to let him forget that he was now a criminal.

Charles' criminal record of Robbery With A Firearm, as well as his alleged confession, were sufficient "probable cause" when he was later charged with the highly publicized axe murder of Jackie Fuss.

Detective Sydney Dorsey handed the Prosecutor a motive for the slaying – an $1800 phone bill that Charles reportedly ran up by calling a phone sex service which resulted in Jackie taking away his phone.

Charles eventually offered his side of the story after he had been sufficiently sedated to calm his hysterical ranting. His lawyer didn't

12

think the jury would buy it, so they never heard what may have been the truth -- that Charles had just come home and was about to take a much needed shower that stifling hot day, so had no clothes on when he went looking for a bar of soap  - in the kitchen pantry where Jackie usually stored such supplies, if you believe the kitchen version, or in the basement if you believe that version.  Discovering his mother dead in the grisly scene, Charles ran out of the house, naked and screaming... and kept running.  Charles' young defense lawyer didn't offer much of a defense at all, other than Charles' obvious mental state. After all, the prosecutor even produced Charles' "*confession.*"

The murder conviction was swift.  Charles was found "Guilty But Mentally Ill" and sentenced to "10 Years To Life." It wasn't until after his incarceration, however, that he was formally diagnosed as being "schizophrenic" and has been in a chemically restrained fog from being forced to take anti-psychotic drugs ever since, so his lawyer did not file an appeal.  The community could rest easy in the belief that justice was served.

It was later rumored that Charles, an easy patsy, may have been framed by one or more of his siblings to prevent him from inheriting. After his incarceration, out of the blue, he allegedly somehow acquired $15,000 that was deposited into a prison account set up for him. Was it a pay-off from the sale of some of Jackie's worldly goods in exchange for his silence? Could he have been framed by the anonymous tipster who had reported Charles "running naked" on the day of the murder?

Charles remains an inmate in the mental ward of Augusta State Medical Prison and isn't talking. Constantly "doped up" on anti-psychotic drugs, poor Charles was described by a fellow inmate as "*mentally gone.*"  Subsequent events would cast doubt on whether justice had been done.

Goodbye, Charles.

Augusta State Medical Prison
Augusta, Georgia

As a side note, on November 30, 2001, Sydney Dorsey, then 61, the detective who gained notoriety for "solving the murder of Jackie Fuss," was arrested for a "murder for hire." The victim was his successful political opponent, Sheriff-Elect Derwin Brown, 46, father of five. The "hit man" opened fire on Brown with a semi-automatic weapon, shooting Brown 11 times in his driveway at midnight as he got out of his car carrying a bouquet of flowers to his wife, Phyllis, to celebrate his election. Also arrested was Melvin Walker, 37, who had been Dorsey's partner on the day they discovered Jackie's body. Until the day of Dorsey's arrest, District Attorney, J. Tom Morgan, who learned that he, too, was on Dorsey's alleged "hit list," had been constantly wearing a bullet-proof vest.

Corruption had a long history in the DeKalb County Sheriff's Department where four of the previous five sheriffs were convicted, charged, or investigated on corruption charges. Despite Dorsey's plea, *"I'm innocent, innocent, innocent,"* on July 11, 2002, he was convicted on 15 charges including Murder, Bribery, Theft and Racketeering. Media reported that he confessed, but he continues to appeal. On the day he was sentenced to "25 Years To Life, Plus 23 Years," the murdered man's wife, Phyllis Brown, reportedly shouted out in the courtroom, *"Praise the Lord!"*

Goodbye, Sydney.

Sydney Dorsey, before and after his arrest

15

Rome News-Tribune - Feb 23, 1989

# Plaintiff in landmark case reverses view on abortion

ATLANTA (AP) — Sandra Cano got a surprising phone call last week.

Mrs. Cano, who was the anonymous plaintiff in one of two 1973 United States Supreme Court cases that legalized abortion, said she got a call last week from the daughter she eventually chose not to abort.

The Atlanta woman, who gave up her daughter for adoption 18 years ago, said the caller told her, "This is Melissa — your daughter."

Mrs. Cano said her daughter located her after reading a recent newspaper article about her fight to reopen the abortion case.

Mrs. Cano was Sandra Bensing at the time her landmark abortion case was filed in 1970. She has identified herself as Mary Doe, the plaintiff in Doe vs. Bolton. The Supreme Court's ruling in that case, which struck down Georgia's abortion law, was issued Jan. 22, 1973, the same day the court struck down the Texas abortion law in the more-famous case labeled Roe vs. Wade.

Mrs. Cano, now 40, petitioned a federal court in December to unseal records in her case in order to help reverse the ruling. She has said she now opposes abortion, and has charged that her attorneys and family pressured her into seeking an abortion and filing the case in the first place.

The woman said she decided against an abortion after filing the case in 1970 and eventually gave birth to a daughter, who was given up in a privately arranged adoption.

16

## 2.
## SANDRA
### *AND THE BLOODY ABORTION COMPLICATION*

Sandra Race was born in 1948 to strict Southern Baptist parents. She was the oldest of six children - three boys and three girls. Her father was Native American – a full blooded Mississippi Creek Indian - and her mother was part Irish, Dutch and German. Her father, a sanitation worker, died when Sandra was only 9 months old.

Except for short stays in Dallas and Grand Prairie, Texas, Sandra lived all her life in Georgia. Her childhood memories are those of a girl raised in a small farm setting, awed by the family's chicken sitting on 13 eggs on a freezing winter day and the 13 chicks that briefly survived.

In 1965, when Sandra was 17, she capitalized on her strongest assets – her pretty face, shapely figure and charmingly infectious southern drawl -- to capture the affections of the good looking, sweet talking, Joel Lee Bensing Sr., a part-time construction worker who she had known about a week.

Eleven months later, on May 16, 1966, she gave birth to their first child, Joel Lee Bensing Jr, who she called "Lee." Their daughter, April, was born next in 1967. Sandra said that, throughout their marriage, *"Ma husband was in and outta work, in and outta jail, and in and outta our marriage!"*

So Sandra took a job as a waitress at The Crystal restaurant to support the family, but she was unraveling emotionally. On June 19, 1969, at age 22, Sandra was pregnant again with their third child, Lisa

Michele, and in 1970, while pregnant with Melissa, she finally had enough of Bensing Sr. That's when she approached the Atlanta Legal Aid Society for help in finding a divorce lawyer. Under the circumstances, Sandra's mother wanted her to have an abortion. At the time, abortion was illegal except to save the mother's life, or to preserve her mental heath, if a panel of three doctors and a hospital committee agreed. So Sandra's mother had her committed to a mental institution after conspiring with Dr. Donald Block to arrange an abortion for Sandra.

Sandra explains, *"As if being institutionalized wasn't frightening enough, almost immediately they informed me ah was going to have an abortion! Ah never wanted an abortion!"* But before the procedure was to take place, Sandra escaped and fled to Texas, her husband's home state, and didn't return until she was 7 months pregnant, although media later reported "8 weeks" - in either case *"much too late to think about an abortion,"* said Dr. Block who was on the panel of doctors at Atlanta's Grady Memorial Hospital. He later claimed Sandra *wanted* an abortion, but Dr. Block had no choice but to deliver Sandra's baby daughter, Melissa.

At that time, Sandra's other children, Joel Lee Jr. and April, were still in foster care. Lisa had been adopted out age 6 months via the Juliet Fowler Home in Dallas. Melissa was immediately released at birth for adoption to Jackie and Bill Fuss whose identities would be kept from Sandra even though Sandra had to personally hand them Melissa in the hospital's elevator where she received the envelope containing $200 cash for medical expense that was immediately appropriated by her not yet ex-husband. Because her application for abortion had been denied, under Georgia statute at the time, Sandra was forced to relinquish "her right to decide when and how many children she would bear" and so she was forcibly sterilized after giving birth to Melissa.

Sandra was devastated.

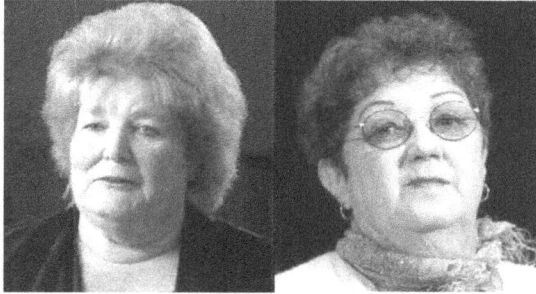

Sandra Race Cano Bensing Domingues Sauceda (aka Mary Doe, Doe v. Bolton, Left) and Norma McCorvey (aka Jane Roe, Roe v. Wade, Right)

Sandra's biological children:
Melissa Fuss Able Erives (adopted by Bill and Jackie Fuss);
Joel Lee Bensing Domingues (multiple adoptions and foster homes;
Joel's photos taken Before & After prison)

Sandra's biological daughter, April Lynn Bensing Egan

While Sandra Race Bensing was dealing with losing her children, her husband was charged with taking one -- a 6-year old child who he was accused of molesting. And in 1971, when Sandra's divorce was finally facilitated by Legal Aid, Bensing Sr., then 23, pled guilty to kidnapping and molesting *3 children* over a 3-month period. He was sentenced to 25 years in prison, where he died in 1988.

Goodbye, Bensing Sr.

In exchange for their services, Legal Aid referred Sandra to Margie Pitts-Hames, an ACLU attorney who asked Sandra to participate in a case they were filing - a case that Sandra only knew "had something to do with women's rights." In the meantime, she re-married in hope of regaining her children.

Sandra explained,

> *"Ah neva testified in that case. At one point ah was asked how ah felt about abortion and ah responded that ah don't believe in abortion and would neva have one. From then on, ah was instructed neva to speak to anyone about the case. Even when ah was required to appear in court, ah was neva asked to testify, just to sit and listen."*

She was picked because the hospital had *denied* her the abortion that her mother and the doctor had sought for her, even though against her wishes, and she was 7 months pregnant when formally denied the abortion. Thus, Sandra says, she *didn't know* that she then became the unnamed woman in the nation's second abortion case to hit the U.S. Supreme Court in 1973 under the title of "*Doe v. Bolton*" - "Mary Doe" being Sandra, and "Bolton" being Georgia's Attorney General, Arthur K. Bolton.

The case reached the Supreme Court at the same time as *Roe v. Wade* -
"Jane Roe" being Norma McCorvey, and "Wade" being Henry Wade,
the Dallas County, Texas, District Attorney who enforced the law
prohibiting abortion at the time, "except to save the life of the mother."
The two abortion cases garnered nationwide attention, while Sandra's
identity was forever sealed in the court record.

For 15 years, Sandra kept the secret as to her role as "Mary Doe" in
*Doe v. Bolton."* But in 1988, when abortion clinics were under siege by
Operation Rescue, Sandra decided to speak out. During that summer
and fall, more than 800 Right To Lifers protested, and many were
arrested in clinic blockades. Sandra said she supported them, but
rather than join demonstrations, she petitioned the court without an
attorney to unseal the records "*...so ah kin get the legal help ah needed to
undo the injustice that was done.*" A judge signed a consent order
opening the sealed file.

> "*Ah can't honestly say what ah understood about the case as
> ah was very naive then,*" she said. "*Ah always knew it was
> something to do with women's liberation. It wasn't until
> 1989 when ah was able to get the case records unsealed that ah
> realized I was used as a test case to enable abortion, despite
> that the hospital only refused to permit the abortion because I
> had already avoided being forced into it by running away
> until it was too late. From then on, it's been my mission to
> get abortion law overturned and save babies.*"

And when Norma McCorvey changed *her* position about abortion
after the *Roe v. Wade* decision, she and Sandra were viewed as
Godsends for Pro-Life organizations trying to get the United States
Court of Appeals to reverse both *Roe v. Wade* and *Doe v. Bolton.*
Sandra's life then became very public. But the abortion complication
and loss of her children were only the beginning of Sandra's troubles.

The worst was yet to come.

Joel Lee Domingues, rodeo cowboy

> *"Caligula and his younger sister, Drusilla,*
> *had an incestuous relationship*
> *'because no one else loved them'"*
> -The History Channel, 2-7-10

## 3.
## MELISSA and JOEL LEE
### *BLOOD RELATIVES, KISSING KIN*

Sandra's daughter, who grew up as Melissa Fuss, always knew she was adopted. But no one would tell her anything about her biological parents, Sandra and Joel Lee Bensing, Sr., nor about her siblings.

Melissa's biological brother, Joel Lee Jr., on the other hand, was adopted three times, his name changed each time – first, by a Mr. and Mrs. Askew who could not cope with the boy who missed his "real mother"-- and then, by Raymond C. Gabriel and his wife who transformed him into Joel Lee Gabriel. Another of his several subsequent foster parents, the Smiths, changed his name yet again.

Sandra also had several name changes – from remarriages. After divorcing Bensing, she married Saturmino Cano in hope of regaining her children. But it was when she next married Fabian Valadez Domingues, that Joel Lee found Sandra. Sandra and Fabian Domingues were able to formally "adopt him back" – Joel's third legal adoption and his third and final name change to Joel Lee Domingues -- the only name he managed to retain but not because he regarded Domingues to be his step-father. Sandra next married her fourth and final husband, Raul H. Sauceda.

Sandra's relinquished daughter, pretty, redheaded Melissa, was 16 in 1987 when she met and married Robert "Bobby" G. Able, 22. They had two daughters, Stephanie and Tiffany. Having children of her own was the first time Melissa had any sense of biological connectedness. Thereafter, she became even more driven to find out about her own origins.

23

In a chance meeting at the Copper Dollar nightclub, Melissa and her biological brother, Joel Lee, crossed paths. Not knowing they were biological brother and sister, they fell in love. That's when Melissa left Bobby.

Jackie Fuss, Melissa's adoptive mother, had always known who was who, ever since the day that Sandra had to hand over Melissa to the Fuss family in the hospital elevator. Upon discovering that Melissa and Joel Lee had been sleeping together, and thinking it was not too late to correct that relationship, Jackie got in touch with a lawyer, Wendell Bard, who contacted Sandra to arrange for Melissa and Joel Lee to meet Sandra so she could *prove* to them that they were biological siblings. But by the time of that confrontation, Melissa was already pregnant with Joel Lee's baby, Vicki, born in 1999.

It's been said that even after Melissa first knew that she and Joel Lee were biological siblings, she kept the secret from Joel Lee. Joel Lee also claimed he didn't know that he and Melissa were biological siblings until well after their daughter was born in 1999.

A record shows that Joel Lee has a low IQ of 73, which was then considered within the range of "mild retardation." Sandra and Joel often said he had been diagnosed in childhood as having autism but that is probably a mis-diagnosis as he did not display autistic behaviors or symptoms. *"But he could be easily manipulated by Melissa's false DNA report."* and that after all the cards were on the table, *"Melissa threatened to kill me."*

On the day of Melissa and Joel's first meeting with Sandra, Sandra had invited Melissa, her then-husband, Bobby, and their two girls to The Crystal for lunch and to talk. By then, Joel Lee knew that he was Melissa's brother and so went along with her to that first meeting. During the meal, Melissa began gazing out a window, distracted by a stray dog she noticed outside. Suddenly Melissa got up and went outside, taking her hamburger with her and offered it to the scraggly animal. Upon returning to their table, Melissa remarked, with a smirk directed at Sandra, *"It's homeless and unwanted.... just like I wasn't wanted,"* just as Margaret used to taunt Melissa when she was a child that she was "unwanted." Sandra quickly corrected her, *"Ah DID want you."* But Melissa fired back, *"Then why didn't you permanently give up April and Joel Lee too?"* *"Because ah had already raised them,"* was the reply. Actually, according to April, who obtained records, Sandra had only briefly regained custody of the girls and returned them to foster care, saying she was unable to handle them.

After an awkward silence, Sandra changed the subject.

Beyond comparing of family resemblances there was so much to catch up on, and so many questions to be answered. To say that Sandra was shocked and at the same time ecstatic to finally see and hug two of her lost children again would be an understatement. Sandra invited them to stay over and they all talked well into the night.

The next morning Sandra couldn't help but notice Melissa and Joel Lee emerging from the same bedroom. Not a word was said about the "kissing kin" at that point, but Sandra later remarked,

> *"Ah thought that was odd, but seein' them was so new and unexpected, ah didn't want to shake the hornet's nest at our first meetin'..."* she explained, *"...still, it just wasn't right."*

For a time, Sandra and Melissa appeared to be getting along despite their unresolved issues. But on November 11, 1989, a *Los Angeles Times* staff writer, Maria Newman, reported that Melissa, then 19, in opposition to Sandra, planned to attend a mass *Pro-choice* rally in Rancho Park. Melissa also sought out and met her infamous father, Joel Lee Bensing Sr., in prison, just before he died. But that meeting was a disaster. She told Sandra that he tried to molest her. *"Now you know why I gave you up,"* was Sandra's only reaction.

25

Eventually, Sandra's frustration from being unable to end Melissa and Joel's incestuous relationship escalated to the point where she complained to authorities. The unintended result was that Melissa and Joel Lee were not only indicted for incest, though never brought to trial, but also all three of Melissa's daughters were taken and placed in foster care.

In a desperate attempt to regain her children, Melissa somehow obtained a DNA test from Tennessee lab where a relative worked, with test results alleging that she and Joel Lee shared *only one* biological parent in common. So she claimed Sandra was *not* her mother, which insulated them from the legal definition of "incest" at the time. When Sandra found out, she was livid, so phoned the lab, insisting that the DNA test results were "fraudulent" and threatened to have the lab prosecuted.

While Sandra maintained that she loved her children, she was angry at the adoption system and the lies and secrecy it spawned, which resulted in the siblings' incestuous relationship.

In a 2007 email Sandra wrote:

> *"Lori, I have been searching for all papers I could find on Lee, and I found a letter from Melissa stating her anger at ma son for not continuing their relationship after he found out they were brother and sister. She says in her letter that she plans revenge."*

.

# Man shoots ill girlfriend, rapes girl, then kills himself

**A life filled with family turmoil ends as he feels everything closing in on him.**

SHANNON COLAVECCHIO-VAN SICKLER
Published August 18, 2004

TAMPA - Robert G. Able started his crime odyssey Monday morning by shooting his ailing girlfriend, once in the head and once in her heart.

Then he lured a 12-year-old neighborhood girl into his home and raped her.

Less than 24 hours later, as police searched the city for him, Able shot himself in the head with the same gun. He died inside a pickup truck at th for the past 16 years.

In between, police say, the 40-year-old former neighborhood crime watch leader visited the Don Garlits Museum of Drag Racing south of Ocala instructions on how to care for the Rottweiler and three mixed-breed dogs he left behind.

Police say Able apparently caved in to the pressures of mounting debt and his girlfriend's health troubles.

Veronica J. Maddox, 40, had diabetes and arterial-venous malformation in her brain, a condition that meant an oversized vein could burst at any

"It appears he just snapped," said police spokeswoman Laura McElroy. Able's family has a tragic history. His father is in prison for molesting Abl who after leaving him fell in love with her biological brother and bore his child. In 1999, she was jailed on charges connected to the fatal stabbing

Tampa police began hunting for Able Monday morning, after a 12-year-old Adams Middle School student told a school resource officer she had friend.

McElroy said Able invited the girl into his house as she walked to her school bus stop. The girl did not hesitate because she'd been inside the tin

Veronica Maddox, Able's live-in girlfriend of 10 years, often babysat the girl, McElroy said. "She considered Veronica a second mother and was

Able took the girl to a guest bedroom and raped her, then drove her to school.

Police staked out Able's house, at 8407 N Huntley Ave., and alerted officers throughout the city to be on the lookout for his pickup truck.

It wasn't until after 8 p.m. Monday, when Maddox's mother and brother went to the house because they hadn't heard from Maddox, that police di Investigators believe she was killed at about 8 a.m. - less than an hour before he raped the girl.

Police found a suicide note in the house. Able spent the first few lines explaining that he killed Maddox "for her own good."

"He said she was better off now because she had medical problems," McElroy said. "He said he was about to lose everything, that he was more

"Then he spent the majority of the letter saying how much he loved his four dogs, and giving instructions on how to take care of them."

At 3 a.m. Tuesday, police discovered Able's body inside a totaled F-150 pickup truck parked at the Bill Currie Ford body shop, 5815 N Dale Mab

After the body shop closed Monday night, Able had parked his own pickup truck next to the F-150. He climbed inside, closed the door, put the gt

In Able's truck, police found a receipt from earlier that day for entry into the Don Garlits Museum of Drag Racing in Ocala.

The museum, with its 300 cars on display, was a favorite haunt of Able's. He apparently decided to go one last time.

Able has no criminal history in Florida or Georgia, where he lived through the late 1980s before moving to Hillsborough County.

He started a neighborhood crime watch group, Southeast Grid 28, in May 2001. It never met regularly, and was officially taken off the city's roste

But Able maintained his interest in law enforcement. In July, he began attending a free eight-week citizens academy offered by the Hillsborough

Able's father, 75-year-old James Able Jr., is in a state prison serving 25 years for the sexual battery of Robert Able's two daughters. Able Jr. was occurred between 1994 and 2002.

McElroy said the state took Able's daughters from him seven years ago, and James Able Jr. took legal custody of them. The girls are now in fost

Officials of the Department of Children and Families would not comment on the case.

Georgia records show Robert Able was 22 when he married Melissa Fuss, just 16 at the time, in DeKalb County. The wedding was on Valentine

In 1991, Robert and Melissa Fuss Able were forced out of an apartment following a landlord dispute, county records show. After that, there is no

At some point, Melissa Fuss Able began a relationship with her biological brother, Joel Lee Dominguez. She gave birth to his child, according to

She later remarried and had three more children. In 1999 she and Dominguez were charged with the murder of the wife of her adopted brother. pleading to lesser charges of burglary in connection with the slaying.

By then, Robert Able had been living with Veronica Maddox in Tampa for five years.

Neighbors said theirs was a quiet life. Maddox, who has adult children living in Alabama, often had yard sales. She went with Able to the car sho

Tuesday afternoon, the back porch light of their house was still on. The screened front porch was filled with lawn ornaments brought in during the

"She was very friendly," neighbor Virginia Ann Roberts said of Maddox. "They did everything together."

Staff researcher Cathy Wos contributed to this report.

Melissa's ex-husband, Robert G. "Bobby" Able, couldn't help her. He apparently didn't see Melissa, nor their daughters, after he remarried and had two more daughters. That family had problems of their own. Bobby's father, James Able, was incarcerated at age 75 in Georgia State Prison for sexually molesting Bobby's two daughters who were then removed from his custody to foster care.

Bobby was 40 and living in Tampa, Florida, when his girlfriend of ten years, Virginia Maddox, had a terminal illness. He evidently "snapped" from worry about mounting debt and his girlfriend's health problems when he kidnapped the 12-year old daughter of a family friend, raped her, then shot and killed Maddox... and himself.

Good-bye, Bobby.

## 4.
## MELISSA, MARGARET, DAVID and JOEL LEE
### *AND THE BLOODY MURDER OF KELLY FUSS*

On June 15, 1999, almost exactly three years after the June 21, 1996 murder of Jackie Fuss, for which Charles Allen Fuss was imprisoned, there was another murder in the Fuss family.

Jackie's other adopted son, David Alan Fuss, a self-employed building contractor like Jackie's husband, told police that he last saw his wife, Kelly, alive at their Stone Mountain home when he left to meet relatives about Jackie's estate which was still in dispute. Jackie had no will, so whatever was left of Bill's estate after her murder might, in normal circumstances, automatically be divided by her children -- children by birth and by adoption -- which reportedly didn't sit well with Margaret, the biological heir.

But the matter of Jackie's cash assets was not be immediately settled by the court, while the siblings disputed who would get what part of Jackie's non-cash assets, including Bill's prized gun collection, still there for the taking.

David claimed that none of the relatives showed up for the meeting about Jackie's estate, so he could offer no proof of his whereabouts that day. He said he returned home and found Kelly slain in a pool of her own blood on their kitchen floor, a hauntingly familiar scene.

Although Kelly Lindsey Fuss, 31, was not slain with an axe, she was fatally stabbed *30 times* in her own kitchen, leading authorities to the conclusion that another Fuss had fallen victim to a "rage killing" by a family member. Charles was in the mental prison so he had to be eliminated.

29

For unknown reasons, David was also ruled out -- despite that he showed no emotion over the loss of his wife and how she died, and despite that a mop and bucket were present at Kelly's crime scene because the kitchen floor had obviously been recently mopped where footprints should have been seen in the blood pools that had trickled from Kelly's wounds. Similar to Jackie's alleged murder scene, there was no attempt to clean the blood found elsewhere in the home, suggesting a hurried, disorganized or interrupted attempted cleanup.

What probably drew attention away from David was a newspaper article the day after Kelly's murder which revealed:

> "*Hours after the murder, Melissa Erives petitioned the County probate judge to allow her to open her murdered adoptive mother's three safe deposit boxes, according to court records.*"

It was then not difficult to allege a motive.

At the time of Kelly's murder, Melissa was married to Romero Ramirez Erives and had three more children. Margaret was still married to David Branch. And Joel Lee was married to Tammy Louise with whom he had another daughter, Jessica. His marriage had to be tumultuous as he still had a bullet lodged in his back *as result Tammy shooting him during an argument.*

According to Joel Lee, on the day of Kelly's murder, Melissa had asked him to drive her and Margaret to David and Kelly's home to try to retrieve guns they believed David had taken from Jackie's home *after* her murder. Joel Lee said he "*waited in the car*" as they asked him to do, while the women entered the Fuss home. He said
> "*Eventually, Melissa reappeared -- covered in blood-- followed by Margaret.*"

Goodbye, Kelly.

But just as there had been different accounts of Jackie Fuss' murder, the Prosecutor's account of events on the day that Kelly Fuss was murdered, as told to police by Melissa and Margaret, were also quite different than Joel Lee's story.

According to the prosecutor:

*"David, Margaret and Melissa quarreled about the distribution of assets in their mother's estate. Margaret and Melissa suspected that David had improperly taken some of the assets for himself. In order to lure David away from his house and give Margaret time to search it, Margaret phoned David and asked him to meet her at their late mother's house. David agreed and drove himself to the meeting place. His wife, Kelly, stayed at home. In the meantime, Margaret, Melissa, and Joel Lee drove to David's house. Margaret entered the house. Joel Lee entered approximately 15 minutes later."*

*Melissa then drove her truck down the street, parked, and waited until Margaret called her on her cell phone and asked her to return to David's house. When she arrived, Melissa saw Margaret and Joel Lee standing on the front porch. Joel Lee drove away in Kelly's car. Margaret got into Melissa's truck and told her that Kelly was dead. Melissa and Margaret followed behind Joel Lee for a short distance. Joel Lee parked Kelly's car, climbed into the back of Melissa's truck and covered himself with a blanket.*

*Forty-five minutes after his departure, David returned home to find Kelly dead on the kitchen floor. She had been stabbed 30 times and two of the wounds were fatal. Blood was found in several rooms of the house. Joel Lee was arrested."*

Joel Lee not only made the mistake of being in the wrong place at the wrong time, with the wrong people, but also, when first questioned by police, he told them *he and Melissa had been together elsewhere at the time of the murder*, in his naive attempt to protect his sister and their daughter.

Authorities said Kelly Fuss' killing stemmed from an ongoing family dispute over the settling of Jackie Fuss' estate. Police initially "liked" Melissa for Kelly's murder, but they had three suspects with conflicting stories, and the D.A. would need to prove which one actually inflicted Kelly's 30 stab wounds.

So the D.A. took the easiest path to a conviction that would put *all three* behind bars, by offering both Melissa and Margaret a plea deal for a lesser sentence -- in exchange for helping to convict Joel Lee. Joel Lee at first denied any part in Kelly's murder but caved when, according to Joel Lee, he was *"threatened into a confession."*

Melissa pled to a lesser charge of Burglary for which she got a 10-year sentence. Margaret pled to Voluntary Manslaughter receiving a 10-year sentence also. Joel Lee's public defender allowed to him to testify at trial instead of requesting a competency hearing to determine whether, due to his IQ of 73, he may not have been competent to stand trial.

Joel Lee, seemingly oblivious to the gravity of his situation, *wrote love letters to Melissa from his jail cell saying he wanted to marry her when they get out* -- which didn't sit well with the jury.

The jury *never saw some of the evidence nor heard witnesses that would have supported Joel's innocence and he was denied a polygraph test*. One of the jurors reported they were being influenced to convict Joel Lee based only on the assumption that he "*was there*" at the time of the murder so "*must have participated.*" Joel Lee maintained that he "*never entered Kelly and David's home,*" but assumed the women went there to reclaim some items and he remained in the car at the time of Kelly Fuss's murder, not knowing a murder was occurring. Still, even as an unwitting getaway driver, he would be regarded as an accomplice under the law. Joel Lee says the 1991 Dekalb County Superior Court transcripts would show the Medical Examiner testified "*a woman did the murder.*"

Despite that Joel Lee insists Melissa was *"covered with blood"* at the time of her arrest, no record of blood typing nor DNA testing is found for Melissa's nor Margaret's clothing or skin.

*One year later,* a pinhead size spot that the Prosecutor alleged was found *inside* Joel's sock that Joel said he had worn *inside his boots* -- a spot too small for accurate DNA analysis in 1991 – was misrepresented to the jury as *definitely being "Kelly's blood."*

Joel Lee's trial commenced on April 27, 2001. Five days later, on May 1, 2001, the jury returned a verdict of "Guilty." Joel Lee was sentenced to 20-Years-to-Life for "Malice Murder and Burglary." His prior 1991 conviction for "Theft and Forgery," for which he served a year in jail, was counted as "aggravating circumstances."

Joel's Habeas appeal (in Domingues v. State, No. So3A1458) was denied on November 17, 2003.

But Joel Lee's story was by no means over.

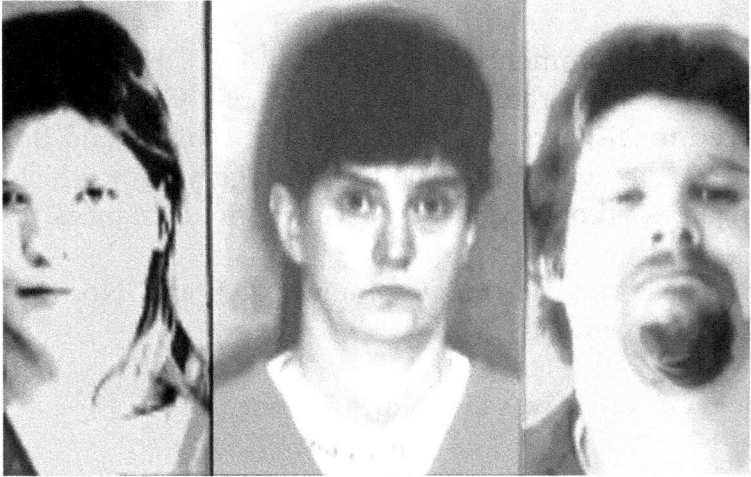

Mugshots:
Melissa Fuss Erives, Margaret Fuss Branch, Joel Lee Domingues

# Supreme Court of Georgia.

## DOMINGUES v. The STATE.

### No. S03A1458.

### Decided: November 17, 2003

Hurl R. Taylor, Jr., Ellenwood, for appellant. J. Tom Morgan, Dist. Atty., Barbara B. Conroy, Rosemary Brewer, Asst. Dist. Attys., Thurbert E. Baker, Atty. Gen., Frank M. Gaither, Jr., Asst. Atty. Gen., for appellee. Defendant Joel Lee Domingues was convicted of malice murder and burglary in connection with the death of Kelly Fuss.₁ He appeals, asserting, inter alia, ineffective assistance of counsel. We find no error and affirm.

Kelly Fuss was married to David Fuss. David was the brother of Melissa Fuss Erives and Margaret Fuss Branch. Domingues was romantically involved with Erives, Kelly's sister-in-law.

David and his sisters, Branch and Erives, quarreled about the distribution of assets in their mother's estate. Branch and Erives suspected that David had improperly taken some of the assets for himself. To lure David away from his house, and give Branch time to search it, Branch called David and asked him to meet her at their mother's house. David agreed and drove himself to the meeting place; his wife, Kelly, stayed at home. In the meantime, Branch, Erives, and Domingues drove to David's house. Branch entered the house; Domingues entered approximately 15 minutes later. Erives then drove her truck down the street, parked, and waited until Branch called her on her cell phone and asked her to return to David's house. When she arrived, Erives saw Branch and Domingues standing on the front porch. Domingues drove away in Kelly's car. Branch got into Erives' vehicle and told her that Kelly was dead. Erives and Branch followed behind Domingues for a short distance. Domingues parked Kelly's car, climbed into the back of Erives' vehicle, and covered himself with a blanket.

Forty-five minutes after his departure, David returned home to find Kelly dead on the kitchen floor. She had been stabbed and cut 30 times and two of the wounds were fatal. Blood was found in several rooms of the house. Domingues was arrested shortly thereafter. A spot of blood on Domingues' sock was tested and determined to be Kelly's.

1.  The evidence was sufficient to enable any rational trier of fact to find defendant guilty beyond a reasonable doubt of the crimes for which he was convicted. Jackson v. Virginia, 443 U.S. 307, 99 S.Ct. 2781, 61 L.Ed.2d 560 (1979).

2.  Domingues asserts he received ineffective assistance of counsel because counsel failed to (1) have the entire trial, including voir dire, transcribed; (2) call essential witnesses; (3) allow Domingues to testify on his own behalf; (4) fully investigate the case; and (5) pursue a hearing with regard to Domingues' competency.

To prevail on a claim of ineffective assistance of counsel, a criminal defendant must show that counsel's performance was deficient and that the deficiency so prejudiced defendant that there is a reasonable likelihood that, but for counsel's errors, the outcome of the trial would have been different. Strickland v. Washington, 466 U.S. 668, 104 S.Ct. 2052, 80 L.Ed.2d 674 (1984); Smith v. Francis, 253 Ga. 782(1), 325 S.E.2d 362 (1985). The criminal defendant must overcome the strong presumption that trial counsel's conduct falls within the broad range of reasonable professional conduct. Mobley v. State, 271 Ga. 577, 523 S.E.2d 9 (1999). The trial court's findings with respect to effective assistance of counsel will be affirmed unless clearly erroneous. Johnson v. State, 266 Ga. 380, 383, 467 S.E.2d 542 (1996).

It cannot be said that counsel were ineffective for failing to have voir dire transcribed because Domingues does not assert that anything harmful or prejudicial transpired during voir dire. See Davis v. State, 242 Ga. 901, 902(1), 252 S.E.2d 443 (1979). Similarly, Domingues cannot show prejudice with regard to his assertions that counsel failed to fully investigate the case and call essential witnesses because he made no proffer as to what a thorough investigation would have uncovered or what the essential witnesses would have said. Roberts v. State, 263 Ga. 807, 808(2)(b), 439 S.E.2d 911 (1994). The trial court found that counsel advised Domingues the decision as to whether to testify was his; that, however, counsel advised him not to testify; that counsel had sound, strategic reasons for giving that advice; 2 that Domingues was fully aware of his rights; that he elected to follow counsel's advice and informed the court to that effect; that the court instructed Domingues he could change his mind and choose to testify; but that Domingues never indicated a desire to do so. Giving due deference to the trial court's findings, we conclude that counsel's advice did not fall below an objective standard of reasonableness.

Finally, we decline to find ineffective assistance with regard to Domingues' assertion that counsel should have pursued a hearing to determine his competency to stand trial. Prior to trial, counsel sought, and was granted, permission to have Domingues psychologically evaluated. The evaluation demonstrated that Domingues was competent. Domingues has not shown that counsel unreasonably relied upon that evaluation.

3. The trial court did not err in charging the jury that whether a conspiracy existed was a matter for the jury to determine. See generally Turner v. State, 275 Ga. 343, 345(2), 566 S.E.2d 676 (2002). The charge did not impermissibly shift the burden of persuasion to Domingues.

4. That defendant was acquitted on the burglary count which was based on an intent to commit aggravated assault, but convicted on the felony murder charge which was predicated on aggravated assault, is of no

consequence. Georgia does not have an inconsistent verdict rule. Hines v. State, 276 Ga. 491, 492(2), 578 S.E.2d 868 (2003). Besides, any error in connection with the felony murder count must be deemed harmless because it was vacated by operation of OCGA § 16-1-7. See Malcolm v. State, 263 Ga. 369, 372(5), 434 S.E.2d 479 (1993); Heard v. State, 261 Ga. 262, 263, 403 S.E.2d 438 (1991).

Judgment affirmed.

FOOTNOTES

1. Kelly Fuss was killed on June 15, 1999. Domingues was indicted and charged with malice murder, two counts of felony murder, aggravated assault and two counts of burglary. Trial commenced on March 3, 2001. Five days later, the jury returned a verdict of not guilty upon one of the burglary counts, and guilty upon the remaining charges. The trial court sentenced Domingues to life in prison and 20 years for the malice murder and burglary convictions; the remaining counts were treated as surplusage and vacated. Domingues' timely filed motion for a new trial was denied on December 12, 2002, and Domingues filed a notice of appeal on January 10, 2003. The case was docketed in this Court on June 20, 2003, and orally argued on September 15, 2003.

2. Domingues gave different accounts of his story when he was interviewed by the police.

THOMPSON, Justice.

All the Justices concur.

*"It takes two to speak the truth;
one to speak, and another to hear."*
-Henry David Thoreau

## 5.
## LAWYERS and LIES
### *AND THE 9 BLOODY LIVES OF JOEL LEE DOMINGUES*

Since 1989, this writer had been assisting adoptees and their unknown biological families wishing to reconnect, without charge, via a national network of volunteers known as Americans For Open Records (AmFOR). As word got around, a number of *incarcerated* adoptees, who wanted to know *their* origins, contacted AmFOR. AmFOR also intervened in behalf of several *wrongfully convicted* adoptees who could not obtain pro bono help from lawyers or Innocence Projects. In 2005, there was an online article about the conviction of Joel Lee Domingues which mentioned his mother, Sandra, and that he was *adopted*. Curious to know "the story behind the story," I wrote a brief note to Joel Lee asking if there was anything I could do for him. He responded immediately:

> May 5, 2005:
> "Dear Lori, I received your letter today and it was surprising to hear that you've read about me in California. Anyways, I am truly grateful for any help that I might get. At the moment I don't need a lawyer. I've got a pretty good one out of Texas and she seems to think that my case will be overturned in about 2 or 3 months on my Habeas Corpus. As you've read, I'm in here for Murder and the sad part is I didn't do it and I didn't know what my two co-defendants were doing.
>
> I know it may seem strange, because I'm here, however if anyone were to read my transcripts they would see that the judge 'had to convict someone.' The judge and D.A. plainly stated that I'm *not guilty of Murder*, however since the D.A. claims there would be questions as to why

they let my co-defendants plea out to 10 years, they let the jury decide. Anyways, for the moment, all I can do is wait, but if you're able, maybe you could help me find my grandfather and maybe a couple other relatives. I don't know the name of my grandfather; my mother will not talk about him. I'm not trying to really know him well, I just want to see what he looks like. Also, I see you offer an Adopted Prisoner Penpal web page. I could sure use a friend. This state has really been hard on me, not to mention my relationships here.

I made really good money when I was out, but it seems like everyone I meet is on drugs and just wants to use me for the money. I'm not a bad person. I worked from sun-up to sundown lugging block and stone and brick. I owned my own home and have never asked anyone for anything. And I don't *look* all that bad. Anyways, if you know of someone who could lend me an ear, have them write to me. Thank you, Joel Lee Domingues."

That Joel Lee had a pro bono attorney to appeal his case was encouraging. I sent Joel Lee a printout of the web page I composed to help him tell his story. It included his photo from his rodeo days that he had provided. He continued to share his story.

June 1, 2005:
"First off, I'd like to thank you for offering your help. That's very nice of you. Second, in my first letter, I should have told you a little about my life. It's true I was in foster care growing up. I thought I had only one sister, April. I never knew Melissa. Me and April were in all kinds of foster homes. We had both been adopted by the same couple and our names changed to Askew, but then they didn't want my sister, and I gave them too much trouble to keep just me, so the Welfare split us up.

Then I got adopted to a family in Louisiana who changed my name to Joel Lee Gabriel. I wouldn't stay because I wanted my sis. So I was flown back to Georgia and placed in another home. I went through hell in all these homes. I was beat and everything else.

I found my mother (Sandra) by accident when I was 13. It was while I was at school and had got into a fight with my uncle who seen my birth name, Bensing, and he told my mother where I was. My mother had to re-adopt me, as if I was never hers, and I had to take the name of her husband at the time, Fabian Valadez Domingues. That guy, Domingues, was a real nightmare. He beat me and her. I had enough of that in foster care so I ran away.

A guy found me sleeping under an office building and helped me. He taught me masonry and I got pretty good at it. It took me just a year to start laying block like a grown man. When I was 16, he went out of business, but got me a job sub-contracting and I made very good money. I was averaging $900 per week. I ended up going back home and run off my mother's husband, Domingues. I had got strong enough to defend myself."

Goodbye, Fabian Domingues.

"We found April through a private investigator. She was living in Washington state under her married name, Egan. Me and April ain't as close as we were growing up, but we are still connected to each other.

Melissa was found by those abortion people. When her and Margaret killed their sister-in-law, Kelly Fuss, I tried to protect Melissa. I said that she was with me the whole time, when in reality her and Margaret went in the house and done the murder. Melissa cried to me, swearing that her sister made her do it, so I believed her. And now I'm here.

I growed up in a living hell, but it really made me strong for the life ahead -- until this. I made a decent life for myself and for my kids. Hell, I bought 3 houses and just gave them to my ex's. The first time I got married, I bought 10 acres of land and built a cabin on it and thought I was in Heaven, but my wife was on crack cocaine. So I made a deal with her -- I took the kids and gave her the house all paid for.

I met a second girl and bought a trailer on 2 acres of land. It didn't last a year and I gave her the house -- she was sleeping around on me.

The third, Tammy, was worse than both of the first two Even though I owned 3 houses, 10 acres of land, had my own business called Family Masonry, she wasn't happy. She spent money like it was water. I was bringing in between $1500 to $3000 a week and yet I still didn't have enough money to buy what I needed and ended up working nights as well, making another $475 per week just to stay away from her, and ended up giving her the house and land and 2 cars. I got blamed for a forged check and she divorced me while I was in jail."

Goodbye, Tammy.

"I'm not guilty of what I'm in here for, and, if you want, maybe I can get you my transcripts. But I think my case will be overturned within a couple more months. I've got a good lawyer that is helping me and she can't understand how I got convicted. She said she will get me out. If I do get out, first I have to get established with money... but then I'm leaving this state."

Joel Lee's letter sounded so optimistic. His attorney, Kathleen Cassidy Goodman, who was not a criminal lawyer, had been assigned to his case on appeal by the Justice Foundation of Texas which then folded due to lack of funding. But Sandra convinced Goodman to continue representing Joel Lee "out of pocket." Sandra was already well known to the Justice Foundation's Allan E. Parker, a Pro-Life advocate who knew of her speaking out against abortion. He had helped Sandra obtain custody of April's two boys, Michael and Joseph, one of whom is autistic. Sandra said that raising her two grandsons gave her a "second chance" to make up for adopting out April, Cindy and Melissa. When Goodman decided to continue to represent Joel Lee on her own, out of pocket, Sandra's knack for getting what she wanted with Southern parlance and aphorisms had reached a new level with comments such as *"Ah'd even be BLACK if it would help ma son!"*

After six months, it was almost expected that Joel Lee's next Habeas appeal would be appealed up from the County Court but it seemed the initial Denial ended his hope.

> On June 18, 2005 he wrote:
> *"You may not want to help me now. I've been in the hospital. I tried to take my life and almost succeeded but somehow I lived. I hung for several minutes. I'm just tired of being locked up for something I didn't do. If only I could get a Judge to read my transcripts, I'm sure I could get out, but I see that won't happen. I don't have any friends -- they left me as soon as they found out I got Life. Some friends! Besides, I'm not going to hang around much longer."*

Horrified that Joel Lee not only had attempted suicide but also implied he's going to try *again*, I immediately alerted his prison staff and Sandra.

My next letter to Joel explained that, for the appeals process, it was necessary that he first be *denied* by the lower court in order to get his case to a *higher court outside the state of Georgia*. I asked him to have *patience* with the legal system and *optimism* for the future.

I wrote him what I had once said to a suicidal, drug addicted adoptee, Noah Stone: *"If you kill yourself today, you'll never know what would have happened the next day."*

What Joel Lee never shared. until years later, was that his depression began when he was first imprisoned -- when he was *gang raped* in his cell by 3 inmates -- and that he lived in fear of other inmates ever since.

I also wrote to Melissa, just once, asking if she needed assistance, stating I help adoptees discover their birth families -- without mentioning that I had been in contact with Joel Lee or had any knowledge of the case. I read that she had been asked by media for an interview about her mother and the *Doe v. Bolton* case but told the reporter *"I'm not that baby. I was raised to believe that I am, but I'm not."* She never replied to my letter.

A whole year passed in which there wasn't much I could do for Joel Lee, except to stay in touch with him, Attorney Goodman, and Sandra. At one point, I located Joel Lee's sister, April, and put them in contact with each other. Then I had an unexpected call... and a visitor. Patrick J. Callahan, Phd, a family and marriage psychologist/ counselor from Los Angeles, having read my book, *"Chosen Children,"* phoned me with regard to my research on *"adoptees who kill."* He said he had served as expert witness in juvenile court cases and had been a consultant in high profile cases such as the Jon Benet Ramsey murder case. He and his wife had a second home in Rancho Mirage, California, just a couple miles from where I was living in Palm Desert, so he asked to meet with me at my home to exchange information for our respective projects.

As result of that meeting, he offered to provide *"pro bono assistance"* to Joel Lee in the form of *"an evaluation report"* including his *"expert opinion"* for Joel Lee's attorney, Kathleen Goodman, and his testimony in court if needed. Knowing how impossible it had been to find lawyers or anyone willing to work *pro bono*, it seemed too good to be true that he dropped in from cyberspace to volunteer. So, as Callahan requested, I put him in contact with not only Joel Lee but also several other incarcerated adoptees, and with Joel Lee's attorney, and with Sandra. Subsequently, Callahan informed me he had traveled to Georgia and met with Joel Lee, Sandra, and Attorney Goodman. Sandra later told me she had objected to Callahan video-taping her and her grandsons without her permission, and would not permit him to interview them "alone" as he requested. She said he seemed *"fishy."*

January 5, 2006, Joel Lee wrote:
"I finally have a court date in May. From my understanding, things look very good for me. If I do get out, I would like to thank you in person for the help that you gave me. Not many people would help someone that they don't know... I figure that if I get out, I'll eat me a big t-bone steak the first chance I get and stay home for 2 days to catch up on some things, then go to work. I'm really good at laying brick and stone. I make really good money at it. Plus, I'd like to find my grandfather and my other sister. Anyways, I'll let you know what happens at Court. I think Dr. Callahan is the main reason things look good."

On September 15, 2006, Joel Lee wrote:
"I'm thankful someone cares, but as for my situation, I don't think they are ever going to let me out. Melissa and Margaret made sure of that when they killed their sister-in-law, Kelly. When I first met Melissa, she didn't seem like she could be my sister. Heck, the first day we met it was crazy. I was lonely and I guess she was too, and she sensed it and got to me. Later, I found out it was all about getting back at our mother, which I don't blame her for, because we all got throwed away like dogs. But Melissa was lucky -- She went to a home that took care of her. Me and April were beat and worse. And we went without eating, no clothes and all. But we had each other. Then they took that away and separated us. Me and April went through a living hell. I still see it

as if it was yesterday. I break down like a baby because I'm so alone. My mother wasn't a mother to me. I was a street kid, always having nightmares, having to fight to cover up my pain. You know, when I first met Melissa, she gave me security and compassion but later she really wanted to use me. I was too stupid to know it..."

Georgia had an Innocence Project but they lacked the funding to help Joel Lee. So, next, we tried Barry Scheck's Innocence Project in New York.

In the meantime, anti-psychotic drugs, including Haldol, were being administered to Joel Lee – *chemical restraints to keep him under control.* The drugs further depressed him and caused or exacerbated his *suicidal* feelings.

> October 29, 2006, Joel Lee informed me:
> "I wrote to the Innocence Project but have not heard anything from them. I haven't heard from them lawyers or Mr. Callahan. Anyways, if you do hear from him ask him if he's going to help me."

> February 26, 2007:
> "I don't know where to turn. I was told that the lawyer that represented me in my Habeas has sent my transcripts to the Innocence Project in New York, yet I have not heard anything from anyone."

Joel Lee was mistaken. Kathleen Goodman said she sent the Habeas Writ but still holds those *Transcripts*, which she would *not* provide to anyone for review *to avoid copy cost* of the voluminous documents. The habeas was Denied as being "out of time to file."

Goodbye, Kathleen.

As for the evaluation report that Callahan alleged he had made, Goodman said she had *paid* Callahan an undisclosed sum, out of

44

pocket, for the report on Joel Lee before Callahan returned to California. But instead of producing the report, Callahan allegedly demanded *more money and refused to hand over any report.* Later, I discovered Callahan was *not licensed to do such evaluations, especially not in Georgia.* I reported him to California's Attorney General, as did a prisoner whose wife allegedly also paid Callahan a large sum. Other inmates who had provided their records to Callahan at his request, complained that Callahan *provided no assistance and neither would he respond to their repeated requests for return of their records.* The Assistant Attorney General came from Sacramento to interview me about it. Months later, they simply closed the Callahan matter.

Goodbye, Patrick Callahan, PhD.

Joel Lee was losing hope:

"I was told I am being helped, yet I don't hear from anyone. I really don't know what to do or who to turn to… As I lay here in my bunk, I think back to all the homes that I have been in and I'm feeling it all over again. Lori, the only way I can get away from it all was beer and weed, and there is none of that here. *The only alternative I have is hurting myself.* I try so hard not to, but my life is so full of pain and misery. You are a very good woman and I'm glad that you are helping me, but if something ever happens to me, I would like to thank you for all our help and of course Mr. Callahan for what he did. I think I made a mistake with the other lawyers. But being it's me, I was too stupid to realize it. Now I'm afraid that no one will help. All my paperwork will be lost in the wind."

Things were rapidly "going south" for Joel Lee. He became despondent *and again attempted suicide by slashing his wrists with a razor blade.* Prison guards and a doctor got to him before he bled out… *But how did he get a razor blade?*

45

Attorney Kathleen Cassidy Goodman (Left);
Judge Linda Warren Hunter (Right)

Attorney Barry Scheck, Innocence Project (Left);
Lori Carangelo, Americans For Open Records-AmFOR (Right)

May 4, 2007, Sandra wrote:
"Lori, I have asked both Lee and the prison warden how my son is able to get them razor blades. Lee will not tell me, other than to say you can get anything you want in prison *and that guards supply it.* The prison said yes, but they have to catch 'em. I also told them that they were failing to protect my son and keep him safe. According to a guard, Lee was also beaten. When I went to visit Lee, the guard on duty said he would make a report but never did. I asked Pat Tyler at the prison why no report was made and she just said she knew nothing about it. Now she does, so I'm waiting to see."

Several of the players in Joel Lee's case had something to hide, and Joel Lee's death would conveniently *"make it all disappear."*

May 10, 2007, Joel wrote:
"I really am at the end of my rope. The reason for my late correspondence is because *I cut myself hoping to bleed out.* I'm just so depressed and you can't really tell the doctor anything because he will lock you down and I've had some very bad experiences locked down... Anyways, thanks again for being there."

May 15, 2007:
"I'm not going to do anything crazy *at the moment.* I want to see how my next court date comes out. It's really hard being here, but I think I can manage a few months more. I'm really sorry I hurt myself. I know that I let you down. It's just that things get so tough to where I can't stand it no longer. I'm not crazy. It may seem like it, but I can assure you that I know everything that I do. When I hurt myself it's because I re-live my childhood and other things every day and it gets to me. I'm sure even the normal person would have a problem dealing with what I deal with. Anyways, I really just want to let you know how really special you are to me and I'm sure

others feel the same way.  I do know David Cassidy who is also adopted.  Me and him are pretty good friends although I never knew he was looking for his mother. I'm glad you helped him and things worked out."

May 30, 2007:
"You asked about Charles.  He's a little off in the head. *When he was on the street, Melissa and Margaret could make him say and do as they wanted.*  Melissa was the prime suspect in Jackie's murder in the beginning, but somehow she got off and Charles became the suspect. *They paid him really well to take the fall. I've seen how much money he still has and it's a little over $13,000.*  He said *Melissa gave it to him.*  Then he said the State gave it to him from his Jackie's estate. I used to be able to talk with him every day til I was moved to a different wing.  Now that I'm back, I'll talk with him some more."

June 6, 2007:
"They really have me messed up. *I'm locked down because I cut myself and lost a lot of blood.*  I've been trying to get information from Charles but it's hard.  He is so doped up he does not know anything.  He talks off the wall. *He did not kill his adoptive mother, Jackie Fuss.  Melissa and Margaret did.*  Matter of fact, Melissa was the prime suspect at one point but somehow got out of it. Anyways, he got *framed* the same way I did.  Lori, I'm sorry that I tried to commit suicide again, but I'm at the end of my rope. I'm trying really hard to stay calm but it's hard to do... I wish things were different. If I get out, I want to just live in the woods away from people."

A July 18, 2007 letter reply from Garland R. Hunt, Esq., Chairman of the State Board of Pardons and Paroles detailed Georgia's parole law.
"Anyone receiving a first time Life sentence for a "serious violent offense" will be eligible for parole consideration after fourteen (14) years.  A Life sentence

for any other offense will be eligible for parole consideration after seven (7) years. A second conviction for any of the 'serious violent offenses' shall be sentenced to Life Without Parole. (Only the second conviction has to be committed after January 1, 1995, and the first conviction could have also occurred in this state or any other state.) The following are designated as 'Serious Violent Offenses': Aggravated Child Molestation, Aggravated Sexual Battery, Aggravated Sodomy, Armed Robbery, Kidnapping, Murder, and Rape.

I regret that I cannot respond in a favorable manner at this time. Sincerely...

After Joel Lee's *8th suicide attempt*, Sandra, with the help of Georgia's Prisoner Advocate who I solicited, finally convinced the warden at Augusta State Prison that they could not adequately care for him and would eventually have a lawsuit on their hands if Joel Lee should succeed next time. We had applied enough pressure to get Joel Lee moved out of state to South Carolina's Columbia Care Center on the recommendation by the Prisoner Advocate that Joel Lee would be better treated there.

> January 10, 2008,
> from Joel Lee while at Columbia Care:
> "I'm doing a lot better. My mind is in good focus. I guess moving me here has done me a lot of good. I'm more relaxed. They have taken me off a lot of the medicine that the other prison was giving me. I guess being doped up so bad hurt more than it helped me. Now it seems as if I'm more at ease with myself. I've got better patience."

August 17, 2008:
"My mind is really going in circles. The State Supreme Court is still looking at my case and have yet to hear it. I've been going to school here, trying to get my GED."

October 16, 2008:
"My appeal was denied and I must say I was very disappointed. I really thought that they would hear my case... I'm just unable to think right now."

November 8, 2008:
"Waiting on the federal courts. Hope I didn't run out of time. I'm sorry for not writing sooner but all the medicine they have me on makes me feel like a zombie. I quit taking it for 2 days now. I'm on Resperdal [Risperidone], Seroquil [Quetiapine], Cogentin [Benztropine], Sinequan [Doxepinhydrochloride] and two others which I don't remember the names of."

The anti-psychotic drugs being administered to Joel produced severe side effects from dizzyness to depression - *including suicidal thoughts.*

February 28, 2009:
"I've been on the downside since the federal court denied my petition. They're saying 'something was not done' before seeking relief from them. I'm having a hard time understanding why my luck is so bad. From the beginning, I was told that the most time I would receive was 5 years. Even the second lawyer said I should have got only 5 years. Instead, I got Life. Lori, it is so hard dealing with this situation that I sometimes feel that I'm going to explode. I'm having medical problems, and I'm just afraid that I'm going to die in here... and I haven't really thought about other people. I've been selfish. I know you and some others have been with me from the beginning."

April 4, 2009:
"I was wanting to get your opinion about my case. I sent the papers to you. I hope you can make some sense of them. I'm at a loss when it comes to stuff like court papers. The lawyers and everyone else said 'the court made a mistake,' yet I somehow figure that I really did 'run out of time.'"

In 2009, prison doctors routinely administered to Joel Lee the following drugs known to have severe side effects: Seraquil (Seroquet), which causes dizzyness, weakness, fatigue; Cogentin (Benztropine) an anti-Parkinson's tremor drug which causes dizzyness, headache, memory loss, nausea; Sinequin (Doxepine Hydrochloride) which causes dizzyness, lightheadedness, drowsiness, confusion... *and heart attack.*

On February 10, 2010, in a last ditch effort, I re-submitted Joel Lee's case to The Innocence Project. A letter signed by Dao Huy, their Case Director, informed us that The Innocence Project of New York again *declined* to assist Joel Lee on the grounds that they believed he was "*a participant in the murder*," despite Joel's defense that he was outside and *never entered* the home *and no evidence placed him at the crime scene.*

On September 13, 2012, NBC TV-26 News and Atlanta newspapers confirmed that authorities caught Marcus Holloway, a guard at Augusta State Medical Prison, bringing to work 3 grams of cocaine and 1/4 pound of marijuana. He was charged with "Intent To Distribute." Because Sandra kept adding money to Joel Lee's prison account, he was easy prey for prison drug dealers and had begun adding street drugs to his daily regimen of anti-psychotic drugs.

By 2013, Joel Lee Domingues, the formerly handsome, blond, young rodeo cowboy, was physically older than his 47 years. He was balding and his teeth were replaced by a denture. He endured nightmarish side effects from the anti-psychotic drugs he was forced to take throughout his wrongful incarceration. *A pacemaker implanted in his chest kept his heart beating.* For 14 years, he had to survive in a prison which was ranked highest in inmate-to-inmate assaults and where guards provided him with razor blades with which to slash his wrists, and with illicit cocaine to dull his mental pain.

Meanwhile, Sandra, navigating in a wheelchair while she looked after her two grandsons, continued to try to protect Joel Lee, even paying extortion demanded by an inmate when he got caught up in a "Green Dot" scam under threat of harm. She also continued to maintain notoriety as to her part in *Doe v. Bolton* and her anti-abortion views, made an online video for Huff Post, and continued to press for Joel Lee's release which she never got to see.

On September 30, 2014, Sandra Sauceda *died.*

She had survived an earlier heart attack and a stroke, but succumbed to throat cancer and heart failure, according to *LifeNews.com.*

Goodbye, Sandra

Joel Lee came up for parole in 2013 and was *denied.* Like the proverbial "cat with 9 lives," he attempted to end his tortured life *for the 9th time....* but *again* survived.

Joel Lee Domingues continued to live from one parole hearing to the next, but when denied parole in 2014, Joel reacted by throwing a chair through a window, his only act of violence during his imprisonment, other than suicidal acts against himself or defending himself against violent inmates. A hearing on the appeal of that denial was anticipated in June 2017.

In the meantime, Joel was especially concerned that a relative of his deceased mother was trying to gain control of Sandra's property -- the home he hoped to parole to -- and they already had one of April's "special needs" sons removed before Joel could "protect" them.

April, who survived much abuse in foster care but fortunately stayed out of the family mess while staying in touch with her sons, Michael and Joseph and by corresponding with Joel, has been happily married and raising her daughter in Texas.

Margaret has not been heard from, her whereabouts uncertain, since her 2007 release from Georgia State Prison.

Goodbye, Margaret.

After Melissa's 2007 Work Release, she lived with David Fuss. David then filed a civil "wrongful death" suit regarding his wife Kelly's murder -- against Margaret and Joel, but not Melissa.

In 2008, David was incarcerated for "Public Intoxication" and again for "Theft/Burglary."

And on September 25, 2011, at age 44, David *died* of an apparent drug overdose.

Goodbye, David.

Melissa then fled to Texas amid speculation that she may have had a hand in David's demise, perhaps for his share of Jackie's estate and drugs, or perhaps to silence him as her partner and witness in the murder of Kelly Fuss.

On May 2, 2014 Melissa was incarcerated as "Melissa Fuss Able" at Randall County, Texas, on drug charges. And that was the last anyone head of her.

Goodbye, Melissa.

MAP DRAWN BY
JOEL LEE DOMINICUS
AS TO PEARL HANDLED
SWITCHBLADE MURDER
WEAPON WRAPPED IN A GLOVE
& TOSSED IN DIVIDERS NEAR A
FENCE, BACK OF SHOPPING CENTER
Note: Covington becomes Hwy 278
& Joel's street. April, results is shopping
center near the former Jackie Fuss house
on Sun Lane. Shopping centers in that
area, today, include Covington Place
Shopping Center and Pedley Hills Plaza
which are next to each other and have
a green area in back.

Joel's Map indicating the location of the murder weapon
used in the murder of Kelly Fuss, the location of
Covington Place and Pendley Hills Plaza shopping centers

54

## 6.

## THE MISLEADING MEDIA
### *AND JOEL'S BLOODY BOMBSHELL*

In 2016, I was contacted, unsolicited, by Nichole Celistan, a producer for Sirens Media production company representing the Investigation Discovery (ID) TV Network. She requested use of "Blood Relatives" as basis for one of ID's "true murder" episodes. When I informed her that Joel Lee Domingues was actually *wrongfully convicted*, I was told they "could only go by the record of his *conviction.*" I responded by refusing to sign a Release or participate *unless* they would allow Joel *his own voice*, either by interviewing him at his prison or by allowing me to express the *reasons* I know that he is innocent of the Kelly Fuss murder. The producers verbally agreed.

Augusta State Prison refused to allow media access to Joel, citing only a vague rule about his "supportive housing" status. Shortly thereafter, he was moved to the non-medical, "general population" at Georgia State Prison in Reidsville -- but it was too late in media scheduling to interview him. There, Joel's counselor reportedly told Joel's sister, April, the reason for the move was "to enable him to participate in that facility's programs for transitioning after parole" and Joel wrote that his counselor "admitted that his previous housing status was *not* the true reason preventing his being interviewed."

Apparently, it was not a security issue that concerned the Georgia Department of Corrections; it was more likely the desire to deflect media attention from corruption that still exists, per the ongoing investigation for several years regarding money scams and drugs supplied to inmates by guards. Later, Joel wrote that Augusta Prison staff required him to sign a statement saying he "did *not* want to be interviewed by media," *contrary* to his and the producer's requests to *allow* his interview.

April was my go-between with Joel, since they had a close sibling relationship and he frequently phoned her on his contraband cell phone. When Joel was moved, his cell phone was confiscated, cutting off any means of direct communication.

In the meantime, Sirens Media producer, Sedg Tourison, flew to Georgia and viewed Joel's trial transcripts at the courthouse. While there, Tourison phoned me stating he had interviewed the original investigator who had doubts about Joel's guilt prior to his trial when Joel kept changing his story as to where he allegedly hid "bloody clothes" never forensically tested after Kelly's murder. In Joel's efforts to deflect suspicion away from his sister, Melissa, Joel had first told the investigator he had "stuffed his own bloody clothes up a chimney" but none were found. He then sent the investigator on another wild goose chase to another location; still nothing was found *because they never existed*. All the Prosecution offered was a single pinhead size spot alleged to be Kelly's blood "inside" Joel's sock over which he wore boots!

By the conclusion of my conversation with Sedg Tourison, I felt that I had convinced him that Joel had been covering for Melissa and was *innocent*.

On April 7, 2016, two Sirens Media producers, including Nichole Celistan, together with their cameraman and two crew members, descended on my home in Palm Desert, California, and set up in my living room for my part of the film's narration. I struggled for the right words as I hadn't slept much the night before, and so Celistan fed me lead-in lines for my on-camera comments. She wanted me to comment about some of the family issues and findings in the Jackie Fuss and Kelly Fuss murders - details not previously available to me, evidently gleaned from producers' interviews with other family members, officials or records. And so, during the filmed interview, I often *declined* to comment about issues I could not confirm or deny, and instead referenced how adoption issues played a part in the two Fuss family murders and how "two-thirds of DNA-cleared exonerations involved false confessions such the false confession by

Joel" -- comments which were *edited out*, but they retained one of my statements:

> "*It was speculated that Charles also gave a false confession under pressure. Due to his mental state, and like Joel Lee, Charles was an easy target for framing.*"

During breaks, Celistan seemed skeptical as to how adoption secrecy can result in murder, so I handed her an article by David Kirschner, PhD, titled "*Violence in Adoption,*" whereupon she acknowledged that she then "got" it.

Again on camera, I was adamant that I believed "*Joel was framed by Melissa for the Kelly Fuss murder*" and that I believed Melissa committed the murder-- because 30 stab wounds indicates *rage* and Melissa, not Joel, exhibited *rage* as result of feeling rejection from being relinquished for adoption and her obsession with acquiring her adoptive mother's estate. All I could do then was wait for the program to air and hope that the program transcript, which would not in itself exonerate Joel, might persuade Joel's parole board to release him or prompt an attorney to intervene.

In the meantime, just before Joel was moved to Reidsville, in April 2016, he dropped a bombshell in one of his brief phone calls to me, informing me that, after the Kelly Fuss murder, in an effort to protect Melissa, *he had hidden "Melissa's pearl handled switchblade knife"* claiming "*she used it to stab Kelly Fuss to death.*" He said he "*hid it at the back of a Decatur shopping center,*" but after so many years, his memory frozen by anti-psychotic drugs, he couldn't remember exactly where.

Over the next few weeks, free of mind altering drugs, Joel's memory began thaw and his revelations flooded my mailbox, including in the form of a crude street map describing the location where the murder weapon, "wrapped in a glove," might be found -- hopefully bearing both the blood of Kelly Fuss and the fingerprints of her actual killer.

I copied April with Joel's letter disclosing the location of the knife, to which she promptly responded:

*"WOW! Last time I spoke to Joel he told me almost word for word what he wrote you... Even if the grocery store is no longer there and it is overgrown, I am sure with a metal detector it could be found. The TV producer was asking me for more pictures if I had them... I have contacted Joel's daughter, Jessica, and she will send me more pictures to give them."*

Why hadn't April informed me about the murder weapon right away? What other "family secrets" were still being withheld from me while I was working hard to try to help Joel?

April said she knew the shopping center he was referring to, and its proximity to the former home of the first one murder victims, Jackie Fuss. A Google map search verified there were still two major shopping centers there, separated by shrubbery - Covington Place and Pendley Hills Plaza - which were on Highway 278 in Dekalb County, the location he and April had indicated.

Rather than jeopardize "chain of custody" by having someone search in the shrubbery on the chance that the knife was still there, I asked Joel to keep this revelation secret until a trusted investigator, or an attorney appointed for his post-conviction DNA testing, could have a *qualified technician* search for it, and, if found, *properly document its retrieval and chain of custody,* and get it to a lab for forensic testing.

At that time, a former Atlanta journalist narrated another true crime story on ID TV, detailing how she solved a murder via forensics. Because she was listed as residing in Decatur, Georgia, I tried phoning her in hope she might help, or get an official to help search for the pearl handled knife. But my phone messages remained unanswered. Neither did a Dekalb County Sheriff's Homicide Detective respond to my phone message requesting guidance in "retrieving a murder weapon in a cold case."

On April 13, 2016, Joel again recounted the events following the murder of Kelly Fuss but with added details:

"The night before the incident occurred, me, Melissa, and Margaret went to David's house. I laid down on the floor board... They made an agreement to meet the next morning at "the estate" [Jackie's house on Sue Lane] at 8 AM. I was supposed to wait inside the Waffle House on [2300] Covington Highway but Margaret said she wanted me to drive her and Melissa to David's house to look for some stolen guns and that they were going to call police if they found them. Hell, I didn't know what they were going to do. They said no one was at home. So I dropped them off and went down the street and parked until they called.

When they never called, I got worried and went back to the house. Melissa came out crying, saying *Margaret made her do it.'* She was covered in blood. From there, *I seen inside the house, and I could see Kelly, or part of her, on the kitchen floor.* Anyways, Margaret came out with some keys and told me to follow her and Melissa. I drove Kelly's red Mustang and they drove the truck.

I pulled into this subdivision, got out, jumped into the back of the truck, but did not cover up like a witness said. We drove back to Margaret's rental car and I got rid of their bloody clothes [in a dumpster] that they changed at the estate house [Jackie's house]. We went to the Waffle House, off 908 Thornton Road in Atlanta, and there they ate like nothing happened and they started talking *about how they framed Charles and that it would be the 'same way.' I didn't know they were talking about framing me.*

Anyways, then we went to pay Melissa's pager bill, just off Moreland Avenue. Margaret took me next door and bought me a black shirt. She said I would be more presentable. Anyways, when leaving to go back to the truck, they started talking about how they were going to make their alibis with the neighbors. When we got back to the truck, Melissa told me to drive around and meet them in 30 minutes, which I did. I went to the storage place off [2300] Covington Highway, and when I finally made it back, I met her on the lower driveway like she said. I called and she seemed surprised which was strange. Anyways, I scooted over and she was driving. When we got on the expressway in Dekalb County, police swarmed in front of us and the first thing Melissa told me was to be quiet. She said there was no evidence and we would be set free within 48 hours... that she's been through this before with Jackie's murder.

Anyways, the lead detective, Harvey, interrogated me and he knew that I didn't kill anyone but he said he was going after Melissa -- *so I said I did it.* After all, I did have a little girl with her. But I didn't know what *she* was telling him.

While in jail awaiting trial, I was getting threatening letters in the mail about hurting my nephew and mother if I talked, *which I showed to my lawyers but they did not look at that.* At first I was scared. Hell, I called my grandmother and told her to tell relatives that I was so sorry, and that I was going to tell the truth. But for some reason, during my trial, Mr. Katz, my lawyer, *would not let me testify, even though at the end I begged him to let me.* Even the other lawyer, Maria Ashley, told him to let me testify. He told me that if I tried to testify he would walk off and I was scared so I didn't say anything... and then they convicted me.

There was a letter that disappeared in a shakedown...a letter that Margaret wrote to Melissa in the county jail, pretty much saying *that they framed poor Charles.* It read *'Keep your mouths shut and no one will go to jail, not Melissa or Margaret, it will just be like with Charles.'*

I had asked Melissa, during the drive to the Waffle House, about Jackie's murder and *she said her and Margaret did it... mainly her.* She wanted the estate. The reason for killing Kelly was because Kelly was fixin' to leave David and they did not want her to get any of the estate in a divorce settlement."

What terrible timing to receive this new version of "Joel's side," detailing circumstances of two murders ... and clues as to the possible location of the missing murder weapon.

Taped interviews for the ID TV were already in production and Joel believed he was being prepared for parole in June 2017 "on condition that he *not* publicly tell what he knew," while a relative of his mother was busily trying to keep him in prison to advance her own interests in his Sandra's estate.

It wasn't long before my silent question was answered in the form of a letter from Joel revealing that the true reason he had attempted suicide in prison, multiple times, was that when he was first incarcerated for this crime, he was *gang raped* in his cell at Hayes Prison. He never reported it for fear of reprisals and had lived in fear of other prisoners all these years.

When Joel was moved from Augusta State Medical Prison to Georgia State Prison at Reidsville, I mailed him a "Motion for DNA Testing and for Appointment of Attorney," under the federal and state Innocence Protection Act, along with an "Affidavit of Innocence," in his Closed Case No. 99CR4217, and a "Request for Trial Transcripts" with an "Affidavit of Indigence" for Joel to sign and return to me, which he did. I then submitted all to the Dekalb County Superior Court, with copies to the District Attorney. I also submitted Joel's Request his request for his prison medical and psych records to his prison's Medical Records Department.

Under the Innocence Protection Act of 2004, the court would have to appoint a pro bono attorney to pursue the matter in Joel's behalf, but only for the DNA matter. The pleadings were duly filed and docketed in early June, 2016. Disclosing even part of the "new information" in support of the Motion for DNA Testing was a high stakes gamble, since it was likely that Joel's "Evidence Box #9092" could have been emptied and his DNA evidence long ago discarded, or it might now be destroyed to prevent testing, but I hoped the filing would tell us either way.

The newly disclosed "pearl handled knife," even if found after so many years, might be too degraded from exposure to be useful as "new evidence," or, worse, it might reveal only Joel's fingerprints or DNA combined with Kelly's blood, from his hurriedly wrapping it in a glove before hiding it. But since he was already convicted of Kelly's murder, we had "nothing to lose." It was Joel's only chance to prove his innocence, so I again pursued the matter of the pearl handled knife by contacting a Dekalb County Sheriff's Homicide Detective, for help in retrieving the murder weapon for forensic testing without compromising the "chain of evidence." But the Detective said they would *not* use their manpower to search for an item that is *"probably long gone, or, if found, any DNA would be too degraded to test."*

On June 12th, a "jailhouse lawyer," housed with Joel, wrote me that he held a Law degree as well as a Masters in Psychology, that he was convicted of a non-violent crime for which he maintained he was innocent, and that he was "intrigued" by Joel and his situation, so offered us assistance. I advised him as to what Motions had already been filed, and on September 12, 2016, Joel's "jailhouse lawyer" filed a "Notice for Judgment by Default" accusing Judge Linda W. Hunter of committing a violation of the Innocence Protection Act and violating Joel's Constitutional right of Due Process by not responding to Joel's Request for his Transcripts, nor his Request for DNA Testing and for Appointment of a Pro Bono Attorney to which he is entitled under the Innocence Act. By law, Judge Hunter was required to respond within the 30-day statutory period but had exceeded that time without response and so apparently was "in Default." However, a "Default" would be meaningless unless Joel's jailhouse lawyer followed up by then *suing* Judge Warren... and that never occurred.

Goodbye, Jailhouse Lawyer.

And that was when, contrary to my instruction to Joel about *not* contacting the Judge, the court Docket revealed that Joel had written *multiple letters* to Judge Linda Warren asking for a "new trial," which according to the jailhouse lawyer, *re-started the Judge's time frame for response, and so she was no longer in Default*. Whether or not any of the jailhouse lawyer's advice was legally factual, on January 31, *2017*, after her 6 months of silence, Judge Linda Warren finally responded by *denying* Joel's June *2016* Request for Transcripts and DNA Testing.

In December 2016, when ID TV finally aired Joel's story, it not only focused on the *Prosecution's theory* of the murder, but also *misled* viewers by having an actor *depicting Joel exiting the crime scene after committing the murder of Kelly Fuss*. Joel's daughter was never interviewed nor even her existence mentioned in the telecast. Joel's and my comments about Joel "*protecting his sister and daughter*" as being the *reason* he signed a false confession, were *edited out*. Neither Margaret, nor Melissa, nor the investigator *who knew Joel was innocent*, were interviewed. Nor was there mention of the several years of phone conversations I exchanged Sandra, in which Sandra told me Melissa had threatened to kill *her* and that she knew her daughter Melissa, *not Joel*, committed *both* the Jackie Fuss and Kelly Fuss murders. It was also *edited out* of the script.

I hadn't heard from Joel Lee since early 2017 but was optimistic that he would be paroled in 2018. And then, in late February, April phoned me with horrific news:

**On February 23, 2018, Joel Lee Domingues committed suicide by hanging himself in his cell.**

Goodbye, Joel Lee. You're finally free of torment. Rest in peace.

Sirens Media producers of Investigation Discovery (ID) TV's
dramatization depicted Joel exiting the crime scene
despite no evidence placed him at the crime scene

# Prison Officials Say Georgia Inmate Died of Apparent Suicide

Corrections officials in Georgia say they're investigating the apparent suicide of an inmate.

**VALDOSTA, GA. (AP)** — Corrections officials in Georgia say they're investigating the apparent suicide of an inmate.

The Georgia Department of Corrections said in news release Thursday that corrections officers found inmate Joel Domingues unresponsive in his cell at Valdosta State Prison around 6:40 p.m. on Feb. 15.

The agency says prison medical staff tried unsuccessfully to revive him and a coroner pronounced him dead around 7:10 p.m.

The agency is investigating, which is standard procedure when an inmate dies in custody.

Domingues was sentenced in 2001 to serve life in prison after he was convicted of murder in DeKalb County.

Corrections officials have previously said that three Georgia inmates died by apparent suicide in January and one other in February, bringing the total to five so far this year.

Sandra, Joel, Melissa, Charles, Margaret

## THEIR BIRTH & ADOPTIVE BRANCHES OF THE "FAMILY TREE" THAT CONNECT TWO MURDERS

## THE MURDER VICTIMS:

### (1) 1996 MURDER VICTIM: INEZ "JACKIE" HYDE FUSS

- JACKIE, whose husband WILLIAM FUSS died in 1993, was the adoptive mother of
- CHARLES ALLEN FUSS, who was found "Guilty but Mentally Ill" after signing a possibly false confession, and convicted of murdering Jackie who was then age 72) with an axe; it is believed CHARLES was framed by his adoptive sisters, MELISSA & MARGARET to keep him from inheriting;
- MELISSA's own mother, SANDRA, accused her of the 2 murders;
- CHARLES was diagnosed as "schizophrenic" after imprisonment for the murder;
- "JACKIE" was biological mother of MARGARET FUSS BRANCH, who resented her adoptive siblings becoming Jackie's heirs; Jackie" was adoptive mother of MELISSA FUSS ABLE (ERIVES) & DAVID FUSS;
- JOYCE BURGE of Cartersville, GA, was 20 with 3 children when she gave up CHARLES & DAVID for adoption because her family could not afford 3 children.

### (2) 1999 MURDER VICTIM KELLY LINDSEY FUSS

- KELLY, wife of DAVID ALAN FUSS who is adoptive brother of MARGARET FUSS & MELISSA FUSS (ERIVES).

67

- The following were originally charged with her murder:
  --MARGARET FUSS BRANCH (convicted of Voluntary Manslaughter)
  --MELISSA FUSS ABLE (ERIVES)  (Melissa turned on Joel, and testified against Joel in exchange for a sentence for a shorter sentence for the lesser Robbery)
  --JOEL BENSING VALADEZ DOMINGUES, (who by all accounts is innocent of the murder - convicted of Murder- Life + 20 Years)

## THE RELATIVES:

- SANDRA RACE BENSING DOMINGUES CANO SAUCEDA (2/16/38 - 9/30/14) aka "Mary Doe" in Doe v. Bolton, abortion case that hit the U.S. Supreme Court same time as Roe v. Wade;

SANDRA's father died when she was 18 & her mother remarried. Sandra's maiden name was RACE;  Sandra had 4 children, beginning with Joel when she was 17; they are:          JOEL,      APRIL,      LISA, MELISSA, by same father, Joel Bensing Sr.

Sandra's husbands were:

- JOEL BENSING JR (Joel Sr. is his father & Joel Domingues is Sandra & Joel Jr's son)
- SATURMINO CANO;
- FABIAN VALADEZ DOMINGUES;
- RAUL H. SAUCEDA.

Joel's bio mother, Sandra, received $625/mo for disability, was raising April's sons, Joseph & Michael, and was sending Joel money in prison.

- JOEL LEE BENSING, SR, Sandra's first ex-husband, is Joel Lee's biological father who in 1971 was imprisoned for kidnapping & molesting 3 children in 3 months; he served only a couple years of his 25-year sentence, died from a brain tumor while driving which caused a car accident. Melissa found her father; Sandra suspected that Bensing Sr. had molested Melissa who told Sandra he attempted to molest her at their meeting years later.
  Joel Jr's Grandfather. also named JOEL LEE BENSING, was last known to reside in a trailer park in a small Georgia town; it's uncertain whether he is still living.

- JOEL LEE (BENSING VALADEZ) DOMINGUES - called "Lee" by his biological mother Sandra Race Cano Domingues;  biological

68

son of Joel Sr.; His daughter, Jessica, by his previous wife, Tami, visited Joel in prison. He & his sister, Melissa, have a daughter, Vicki. Sandra often claimed Joel was autistic but he did
not have Autism Spectrum Disorder behaviors or symptoms; his attorney argued that Joel was naive and was used by Melissa as a pawn in the murder, as Joel has an IQ of 73.
Joel's name was changed several times by several foster parents: His birth name is JOEL LEE BENSING JR;
first changed by his first adoptive parents Mr. & Mrs. ASKEW; then by his next adoptive parents, the Raymond C. GABRIELs, and probably again changed in foster care and then to SMITH; and then adopted by biological mother SANDRA DOMINGUES and her then-husband, Fabian V. DOMINGUES;
Attorney Kathleen Cassidy Goodman, formerly of Justice Foundation of Texas, who was not a criminal defense lawyer, tried unsuccessfully to appeal Joel's conviction, pro bono.

- MELISSA FUSS ABLE (ERIVES)

biological daughter of Sandra Cano, bio sister of Joel, although when the County took Melissa's children to foster care and threatened to arrest them for Incest and negligence, Melissa produced a DNA test from Kentucky alleging she and Joel were not biological brother & sister; Sandra, who reported the two to authorities for being in an incestuous relationship, maintained that the Kentucky DNA test result was a fraud--that they are full brother and sister. Melissa & Joel had a daughter together -- Vicki. were indicted for Incest in 1999 but never convicted & reportedly Joel did not know Melissa was his sister due to being adopted separately, and not until well after their daughter Vicki was born; it's unclear when Melissa knew. Melissa has 2 other daughters, Stephanie & Tiffany, by Bobby Able. Sandra feared Melissa would carry out her threat to kill her & had attempted to in the past and states Melissa was sent to a reformatory by her adoptive mother, Inez ("Jackie") Fuss, for allegedly prostituting at age 9 and was not permitted to be in certain areas of the house, while Jackie's husband was made to live in a trailer outside the

- APRIL LYNN BENSING EGAN-

Biological daughter of Sandra Cano, bio-sibling of Joel, was adopted separately from Joel. April has 2 developmentally disabled children,

Joseph & Michael, raised by her mother, Sandra with "special needs" funds. April, happily married, also has a daughter who she raised.

Their Children:
- JESSICA - Joel's, and previous wife Tami's, daughter who initially visited Joel in prison.
- VICKI - Joel's & Melissa's daughter who was placed in foster care.
- STEPHANIE - Melissa & Bobby Able's daughter
- TIFFANY - Melissa & Bobby Able's daughter

William Edward Fuss, 1921-1993, and
Inez Hyde Fuss ("Jackie"), January 4, 1925 – June 21, 1996,
graves at Forest Hills Memorial Gardens,
Forest Park, Georgia

# ADDENDUM
## ABOUT WRONGFUL CONVICTIONS

*"Wrongful convictions happen every week*
*in every state in this country.*
*And they happen for all the same reasons..."*
-John Grisham

Since 1989, more than 2,200 people in the United States have been exonerated of serious crimes, according to the first National Registry of Exonerations, a joint project of the University of Michigan Law School and Northwestern University School of Law. **False accusations and deliberate mis-identifications were most often the cause**.

*More than 2/3 of the DNA-cleared homicide cases documented by the Innocence Project were caused by false confessions.*

Many false confessions somehow contain details matching crime details that had not been made public.

*Eyewitness identifications are wrong about 50% of the time.*

Particularly for people like Charles Allen Fuss and Joel Lee Domingues, who are unable to represent themselves, or to find a competent criminal appeals attorneys willing to represent them pro bono, proving innocence post-conviction is impossible.

Even with help of this writer in communicating the plight of Joel Lee Domingues to Georgia's and New York's Innocence Projects, and to Southern Poverty Law Centers, these organizations based their refusal to assist him, in part due to "funding limitations" and in part due to their requirement that the wrongfully convicted person "must not have *participated* in the crime" which they decided to believe is true in Joel Lee's case by relying on the false record. Although I obtained certain records, news accounts, and corroborating interviews, I was refused certain police reports despite Joel Lee's signed Release authorizing me to obtain them.  According to his Appeal, it was claimed that the Court "failed to have transcripts made of his trial," at least not immediately after trial, which also prevented his Due Process.

For years, Joel Lee's mother, Sandra, and I worked in concert to get Joel Lee better care to keep him alive. According to Sandra, and the advice she was getting from one of his keepers, the Parole Board wanted to hear *remorse,* not that Joel Lee was *"wrongfully convicted,"* and *"to see if he becomes suicidal if denied parole"* - an absurd and cruel "test" *to determine whether he's too unstable to be released by telling him he won't be released!*  Sandra's influence over her boy's decisions had always been strongest, even when he had an attorney, and it was unlikely that he would disobey her instructions except whenever denials of his appeals, coupled with depressive side effects of prescribed drugs, caused him to attempt suicide.

Even before their years of imprisonment and chemical restraints, Joel Lee and Charles had been psychologically damaged by the emotional abuse inherent in America's adversarial closed adoption system. Despite a steady decrease in closed adoptions, in favor of open or semi-open adoptions in some districts, the unhealthy secrecy in closed adoption is still advocated by Child Protective Services (CPS), family courts, and a powerful a lobby of Christian adoption agencies under the umbrella of National Council For Adoption, all of which profit from federal and state funding under the Adoptions and Safe Families Act by removing children from their parents – parents never determined to be unfit -- and funneling the kids through the current multi-billion dollar American adoption industry to a fate that no social worker can predict nor guarantee, by promoting a "culture of adoption" with only a "positive" picture of adoptees' outcomes. NCFA partners with major corporations -- including WalMart and Wendy's -- to further that goal.  In the documentary, *"Chosen Children 2019 (People As Commodities In America's Multi-Billion Dollar Failed Foster Care, Adoption and Prison Industries)"* this writer follows the dollars and the special interests, detailing the process.

Incest among adoptees who did not know of their biological relationship is an issue in Joel Lee's story. Winona Durbin, former California adoptions social worker for Riverside County, and others, cite "adoption incest" as being more prevalent than the general public is aware.

Psychiatric drugs are over-prescribed to children for behavior modification or to more easily warehouse and forget them. Psychologists cite an "over-representation" of adoptees in therapy for behaviors some characterize as "Adopted Child Syndrome."

And above all, for many wrongfully convicted denied post-conviction DNA testing or whose conviction for murder or other felony did not involve DNA evidence, a better system for reviewing cases of those claiming innocence is needed. Children continue to stream through the revolving doors of America's symbiotic failed foster care, adoption and prison systems, including those wrongfully convicted, in ever increasing numbers.

## ADOPTION-LINKED SUICIDES

In a study of suicide rates among adoptees versus children raised by biological parents, the mean age of the 1000 participants was about age 14;  56 had attempted suicide; 47 of those were adoptees.

**The odds of a reported suicide attempt were <u>4 times greater in adoptees</u> compared with non-adoptees (odds ratio: 4.23)** - (Source: Margaret A. Keyes, PhD, et al, *"Risk of Suicide in Adopted and Nonadopted Offspring,"* Journal of the American Academy of Pediatrics, Oct. 2013, 132(4) 639-646).

Adoptees are more likely to have difficulties with drug and alcohol abuse, as well as eating disorders, attention deficit disorder, infertility, untimely pregnancies *and suicide* (Young, Bohman, Mitchell, Ostroff, Ansfield, Lifton, Schecter).

**141 of 147 suicides involving drugs, from 1983 to 1993, were by Adoptees.** (Source: Brother Alex McDonald, Jesuit Priest, Youth Worker, Melbourne, Australia, 6-3-93)

**In America, *attempted* suicide and *actual* suicide**
**are more common among adolescent adoptees**
**than those who live with biological parents.**

In *"Psychiatric Illness,"* Mary Bohman researched adults adopted as infants. Her 1979 study of 2,323 adoptees revealed an over-representation of alcohol, drug abuse and personality disorders in both male and female adoptees and a high risk of **suicide**. It bears repeating:

*"There is no formula for making a stranger's child*
*live up to their adoptive parents' expectations.*
*To a child, the burden of such expectations*
*translates as abuse."*
--Center for Adoption Support and Education (CASE).

A national longitudinal study was conducted of 7th and 12th grade students, in which adoptees were found to differ significantly from non-Adoptees (Source: Gail Slap, MD; Elizabeth Goodman, MD; Ben Huang, MS-Pediatrics, in the Official Journal of Pediatrics, Vol, 108, No, 2, 8-1-01, p2)

Males, more often than females, have indicators of social maladjustment. Moreover, epidemiological studies show high levels of psychiatric illness, addiction, criminality and **suicide** compared to the control groups. The odds ratio:
**3.2% - in psychiatric hospital care**
**2.6% - in treatment for alcohol abuse**
**5.2% - drug abuse**
**2.6% - severe criminality leading to imprisonment stood**
**3.6% - suicide attempt.**
(Source: *Tranracial Abductees* web-site transracialabductees.org/)

Yet females, more often than males, have shown indicators of poor mental health. A record high odds ratio of 5.0 for **suicide** rates in the U.S. compared to ethnic Swedes, in an international perspective only comparable to the staggering **suicide** rates registered among indigenous people in North America and Oceania.... which makes parallels to cultural genocide ghastly topical. Source: *"Transracial Abductees - Outcomes of Intercountry Adoption"* -by Tobias Hubinette

**MELODY DILORENZO**. At age 24, **adoptee**, Melody DiLorenzo, was hospitalized in critical condition from multiple stab wounds allegedly inflicted by an assailant as result of a drug deal gone bad. (*"Desert Hot Springs Woman Stabbed,"* by Stephanie McKinnon, Staff Writer, The Desert Sun, 8-7-93). But Sheila Grove, Melody's adoptive mother, said Melody's wounds were self-inflicted – one of several

**suicide** attempts of the past three years (*"Why I'm Anti-Adoption"* by Sheila Grove). From her hospital bed, Melody told me she wanted to find her natural mother. By pulling some strings, mother and daughter were reunited within 24 hours and began a long healing process. (Source: Medody DiLorenzo and Sheila Grove)

**NOAH STONE.** Noah Stone was born August 1, 1958, to 17-year old Jackie Sue Owens. In 1962, when Noah was 3-1/2 years old, his father, Kenneth Eugene Owens, sold him to Herbert and Gladys Gill for $350 at a bar in Huntington Beach, California, known as the "8 Ball Cafe." The Gills later "legalized" the **adoption** and renamed the boy Herbert Kent Gill, who, in adulthood, changed his name to Noah Stone in order to "have a name of his own. Noah had attempted **suicide** several times while on drugs. Noah believed, as the theme song from the long running TV series "M.A.S.H." alleged, that "suicide is *painless,*" or at least would end his lifelong painful torment. I reunited Noah with his mother, Jackie Sue, and sister, Susan, during his parole hearing at Arizona State Prison in Florence, Arizona.

**KAREN ANN QUINLAN.** Karen Ann Quinlan, an **adoptee**, made national headlines when she fell into a coma for 10 years from over-dosing on drugs and alcohol. Her journal reflects possible thoughts of **suicide**: *"I wish to curl myself into a fetal pose and rest in the eternal womb awhile."* Society became distracted by the legalisms surrounding whether Quinlan's life support machine should be disconnected and whether she had "the right to die with dignity." The question as to whether adoptees like Quinlan have the right to life with dignity, from knowing their own origins, was never mentioned. (Source: *"Karen Ann Tells Her Story,"* Doubleday, 1977).

**JOSEPH JOHN CANNON.** At ages 7 to 8, Joseph John Cannon was sexually abused by his **adoptive** father (his mother's 4th husband) and regularly sexually assaulted by his grandfather from age 10 to 17 when he was diagnosed as suffering organic brain damage from sniffing glue, solvents and gasoline, and was schizophrenic. He was treated in psychiatric hospitals for these conditions and for severe depression. At age 15 he attempted **suicide** by drinking insecticide.

At age 17 he was tried as an adult for the 1977 murder of Anne Walsh. By the time he was executed in Texas in 1998, Cannon had learned to read and spent more than half his life on Death Row. (Source: Amnesty International document, USA [Texas] *"Death Penalty, Legal Concern: Joseph John Cannon,"* AMR 52/13/98, UA 80/98 2-26-98)

**TIMOTHY JASON JONES**. Born 6-23-75, in Alabama, Timothy Jason Jones, 29, murdered his **adoptive** parents, Nancy and Timothy Jones, in January 2004. He committed **suicide** at Holman maximum security prison. (Source: Connie Baggett, Mobile Register Alabama 9-3-06 )

**CHARLIE LITTLE JR**.    Born Alexander Julian Morgan, in 1984, Charlie Little Jr. killed his **adoptive** parents, Arlene and Charles Little Sr., with a shotgun and tried to cover it up as a burglary gone wrong. According to his teachers who testified at his trial, in his writing classes at school, Charlie Jr. was known to turn in very graphic, disturbing and violent stories that freaked out his teachers. At his trial, the Judge had to throw out key evidence such as shotgun residue discovered on Charlie Jr's hands, so he was *not* convicted. Little later changed his name to his birth name, Alexander Morgan, and moved away from Iowa. In 1992, in Tennessee, he committed **suicide** by driving his car into a wall at high speed (Source:  Iowa v. Alexander Julian Morgan, 1986).

**CASEY BROOKS.**   In 2013, John Brooks wrote an article about his **adopted** daughter, Casey Brooks, and the issues inherent in intercountry adoption, after the teenager committed **suicide** by jumping off the Golden Gate Bridge in San Francisco (Source:  John Brooks, *"Adoption and Suicide:   Casey's Story,"* Adoption Voice Magazine, 9-14-13).

**KOREAN ADOPTEES.**   Critics claim Korean adoption agencies established a system to guarantee a steady supply of healthy children. Korean and other international **adoptees**, even more than domestic adoptees, are highly over-represented when it comes to *suicide*, **suicide attempts,** mental illness, substance abuse, crime, social maladjustment, and other issues (Hjern et al, 2002).

**ANDREA SWENSON.** Andrea was 9 years old when she committed **suicide** in Oklahoma. When the Swenson's insurance ran out that had been covering Andrea's $3500/week therapy, the "Attachment Center" pressured her adoptive parents to allow the Center to *adopt* Andrea and thereby get new insurance coverage. When told of the scheme, Andrea committed **suicide**.

**ASHLEE BUNCH**, Ashlee was **adopted** at age 4 by a divorced man who remarried and sent Ashlee to McGraw Residential Center with multiple diagnoses of Attachment Disorder, Bipolar Disorder, Fetal Alcohol Syndrome effects, Attention Deficit Disorder, and Defiant Disorder. By age 15, she attempted **suicide** 8 times. While at a **suicide prevention center** in Seattle, on January 28, 2008, Ashlee *successfully* hanged herself to death with a shoelace.

**JOSEPH KALINGER.** He was born December 11, 2003, as Joseph Lee Brenner III, to Joseph and Judith Brenner in Philadelphia. His father abandoned the family in 1937, which is when he was first placed in a severely abusive foster home. He was then **adopted** by Stephen and Anna Kallinger, a sadistic Catholic couple who beat, burned, and starved him. He abused his 2 wives and 5 children and killed his own son for insurance money. After beheading his adoptive mother, he raped her headless body. He was in and out of mental institutions for **suicide attempts** and for setting his house on fire 3 times. A cobbler by trade, he sexually tortured a family and murdered 3 people. In prison, he was diagnosed as Paranoid Schizophrenic and *repeatedly attempted to kill himself,* including by setting fire to his cell. In later years, Kallinger expressed remorse, refused to eat, and **attempted suicide again.** On March 26, 1996, at age 59, after 11 years on **suicide** watch, he died in prison of an epileptic seizure (Source: "Crime Library," and Wikipedia).

**MICHAEL OSMOND**. Michael was one of 5 children **adopted** by Marie Osmond. At age 18, he committed **suicide** by jumping to his death from his downtown Los Angeles apartment after Marie and her husband, Brian Blosil, split up (New York Daily News, 2-28-10).

**BILL BERLE.**  Born in Rome, Italy, in 1961, Bill was **adopted** when he was 6 days old by famed comedian, Milton Berle, to please his wife, Ruth, who was infertile.  I met Bill while autographing and promoting *"The Ultimate Search Book"* at the same Barnes and Noble Book Store in Palm Desert, California, where Bill was autographing and promoting *"My Father, Uncle Milty."* During our brief chat, he alleged that he *"wasn't interested in finding his biological parents because the Berles were his parents and that he had a happy life"* ... which was coming from the perspective of someone raised in Beverly Hills among celebrities, affluence, glitz and glamour.  The truth was that his black market adoption left no paper trail and according to Bill's own  biography, *"My Father, Uncle Milty"* (on Amazon), he describes Milton as someone he hardly knew who was always on the road in show biz and never paid much attention to him... and that an argument he had with Milton that ended with Milton shouting that he *"wished they'd never adopted him,"* Bill "snapped" and was about to commit **suicide** but was interrupted as he was reaching for the gun.

**MARILYN MONROE.**   Born to a single mother, and named Norma Jean, she was fostered from infancy til age 2, and, although she had contact with her mother, she did not know who she was after being adopted by her mother's best friend.  The **adoption** was annulled or ended by returning her to a series of 9 foster homes. Marilyn married at 16 to get out of foster care, abused pills and alcohol, was mistress to President John Kennedy and his brother Robert, as well as to a Mafia figure. Her early death has been attributed to **suicide**, accidental overdose, *and/or* a Mafia murder conspiracy during the Kennedy years. (Source: her own book and Wikipedia.

**AILEEN PITMAN WUORNOS.**  A former foster child, **adopted** as an adult in 1978 at age 22, and a convicted serial killer, shot herself in the abdomen.  She told emergency room doctors *it was not the first time she* attempted **suicide**, yet received minimal psychiatric care. She also halted all appeals of her Death sentence, in effect a "legal" **suicide**. (Wikipedia)

Bill Berle and Lori Carangelo talked about his **adoption**
while promoting their respective books.
His book revealed he had attempted **suicide**.

**EVAN RAMSEY.** Born in 1981, "the Alaska School Shooter," Evan Ramsey, went through a series of foster homes because, at age 7, his father went to prison and his mother became an alcoholic. In one of those homes, he was sexually abused. On February 19, 1997, when he was 16, he walked into his school in Bethel, Alaska, pulled out a .12 gauge shotgun and murdered 2 people. Then Evan put the gun under his chin. But he never fired the final shot. After a short standoff with police, he surrendered and was convicted of Murder and Assault. *"My main objective in going into the high school was to* **check out**," he said… *"to commit* **suicide**." Up to that point, Evan had a difficult life. Psychiatrist, Dr. John Smith, who examined Evan after the murders, found that Evan had attempted **suicide** at age 10. According to Dr. Smith, Evan was depressed from a young age. By teenage, he was using marijuana, getting poor grades and struggling to control an explosive temper — as an outsider, someone who didn't fit in with the athletes and popular kids at school. He was sentenced to 200 years in prison and will be eligible for parole when he's 75. (Source: CBS-60 Minutes, 3-7-01, and court testimony.)

**OTHER SCHOOL SHOOTERS.** It is noteworthy that most "school shooters" are **adopted**, or have had a family separation resulting in circumstances similar to those associated with adoption. **Suicide** during the killings may or may not have been planned, but also the result of finding no satisfaction from the killing, but rather, the murders and the suicides are often triggered by a "secondary rejection" of some sort -- second to being given up for **adoption**. (Michaud, 8-25-99)

**DAVID WAYNE CASSADY.** David revealed "I did contact my biological mother by mail and she then wrote back. However, she has said some things I did not like. One was that she would never have 'allowed' me to come to prison and that she was going to change my (gay) lifestyle. First of all, my **adoptive** mother did not "allow" me to come to prison – I put myself there. She has been loving and supportive. And if my real mother wants to change my lifestyle, she needs to go back 40 years to do that. I don't write her any longer. I will wait til I'm released to talk face-to-face. I'm thankful for your help. I needed to know who she is. I've been on CSU (mental health lockdown) because I tried to commit **suicide**. (David Cassady's correspondence with Lori Carangelo.)

**JACK UNTERWEGER.** Born 8-16-50 in Austria under the name, Johann Unterweger, he was abandoned by his mother, a prostitute, who left him with her alcoholic father and an aunt who was also a prostitute. His father, Jack Becker, an American soldier born in the U.S., also deserted him. Unterweger murdered prostitutes in Los Angeles and in Austria and received his first Life sentence at age 25 when he strangled a prostitute with her bra because she *"reminded me of my mother... I envisioned my mother in front of me, and I killed her."* Hailed as a model for rehabilitation, Jack was granted parole in 1990. Within months of his release his success as a writer translated into expensive suits, fancy cars, and regular appearances on local talk shows, but he kept up his old habit of strangling prostitutes for kicks, leaving at least 6 dead. In 1991 he was hired to write an article about prostitution in Los Angeles. While on assignment he got to travel in an LAPD patrol car and murdered 3 prostitutes before returning to Vienna. By February, 1992, he was wanted for the murders of 8 women, but escaped with his 18-year-old girlfriend to Switzerland, Paris, and New York, pausing to call newspapers and talk shows in Austria to proclaim his innocence. Unterweger was eventually deported back to Austria where he was indicted for the murders of 11 prostitutes, including 3 from Los Angeles. On 6-28-94 a jury in Graz, Austria, found him guilty of 9 of the murders. Soon after sentencing in 1992, Unterweger used the string from his prison jumpsuit to commit **suicide** by hanging himself. (Source: *"Jack Unterweger Biography,"* Biography.com, and related articles)

**RUSSELL MANNEX.** Russ wrote: "I was **adopted** at the age of 2 months and know absolutely nothing about my biological parents except for their nationality. According to the adoption agency, my mother was too young to raise me and her conservative family believed the best option was to send her to a convent and allow me to be **adopted**. My dad is East Indian and my mom is 1/4 Italian and 1/4 Irish. I've tried to make sense as to why I did not feel loved by my adoptive parents. I ran away from home at age 5 because of physical and emotional abuse as result of their alcoholism and not considering me one of their own. I felt unloved, unworthy, guilt, shame, anger, resentment, fear of abandonment, rejection, denial and distrust, all at the same time. By age 8, I began serious lying and set a field afire which was only a hundred yards from our house. I wanted to "belong," and tried to cloud my feelings. If I would just hint that I wanted to know about my biological parents, I'd get a negative reaction. I began to use and sell marijuana, and, at age 16, I attempted **suicide** by swallowing 40 Valium pills with turpentine. But before I could completely load my shotgun to finish the job, I passed out and awoke in a Detention Center, where I self-inflicted stab wounds and refused to eat. I was ordered by the court to see a psychologist for six months. But within a couple months, the psychologist—the first person I had begun to trust—molested me. Shortly afterward, a teacher and a friend of the family both molested me. In 1994, I began this sentence of 7 to 15 years for Attempted Rape. Since late 1997, I have been a cancer survivor in search of my past—still trying to fill an empty hole. God help me. Then one day my biological mother and my brother (her other son) found me through AmFOR's Adopted Prisoners website. Finally, I heard a Texas accent on the phone and we've been in communication ever since. At first, she had some difficulty with my being Gay. But we are hoping I can go to Texas to visit her when I'm out, or possibly even transfer my parole. Connecting with my mother has changed my life. The only 'loose end' is finding my father, Thomas Phillips Smith. I hope to someday finally meet him. Thank you for your help over the years. You have given me a beautiful gift." Russ shared that he is writing a book about his life, titled *"Rocket Man."* In 2010, I was surprised to receive an e-mail from Russ informing me he had been released from prison, was looking for work, and hoped to visit his mother in Texas when he could afford to. I didn't hear further until 2011 when his adoptive mother, Lorraine Mannex, phoned me to thank me for helping Russ find his natural mother. She said it has had a positive impact on his life and that all was going well for Russ. (Russell Mannex's correspondence with Lori Carangelo)

**JACK WESBECKER.** Born in 1942, Wesbecker never knew his father who died when he was 1 year old, and he had difficult childhood with his 16-year old mother, Martha. He was, at first, fostered by relatives, but ended up in an orphanage. As an adult, he took up a trade as a printer, had 2 failed marriages, and in 1988 was prescribed Prozac for depression. He began to talk about fantasized sexual abuse, made a **suicide** attempt, and was put on a number of other medications, then again given Prozac. On September 14, 1989 he went on a killing spree with an AK47 and other guns at his work place, the Standard Gravure printing plant in Louisville, Kentucky, killing 8 of his former colleagues, severely wounded others, before committing **suicide** by shooting himself to death. (Source: *"Fentress et al v. Shea Communications."*)

**SUICIDAL MOTHERS.** Psychologists have recognized that mothers who relinquish children for **adoption** suffer lifelong psychological consequences. (Source: Mary Olsen Wiles and Amanda L. Badem, Counseling Psychologists, *"Birth Parents in Adoption: Research, Practice and Counseling Psychology"* Montclair University, 2013 Journal Citation Reports, Thomson Reuters 2013). Postpartum Psychosis is a separate mental health issue, sometimes erroneously referred to as Postpartum Depression. It is less common than PPD, and it involves the onset of psychotic symptoms that may include thought disturbances, hallucinations, delusions and/or disorganized speech or behavior, homicidal or suicidal thoughts, often resulting in attempted or actual murder or **suicide.** The prevalence of Postpartum Psychosis in the general population is 1–2 per 1,000 childbirths, however the rate is 100 times higher in women with bipolar disorder or a previous history of postpartum psychosis. **Out of 54,000 births over a 12-year period, psychiatric admissions were 7 times more likely in the first 30 days after childbirth than in the pre-pregnancy period** (Source: *Wikipedia*)

> *"The young woman with poor self-esteem and low assertiveness may take decades or forever to drop her denial and collusion with the beliefs pedaled by the adoption agency."*
> (Source: Geoff A. Rickarby, MB, BS, psychiatrist)

**CINDY JORDAN.** Jordan committed **suicide** after losing her daughter to a "fast track **adoption**" in New York. (Source: *"Fast Track Adoption Ends in Suicide,"* PRWeb, 4-13-04)

**ANNABELLE MORRIS.** Morris was a 19-year old with a number of problems relating back her having been neglected in childhood. The psychological effects of neglect, as a child in care herself were then used as "evidence" for the forced separation and **adoption** of her daughter. Sadly, this type of scenario is utilized every day in U.K. and U.S. family courts. Social Services uses the secrecy of the family courts to needlessly remove children from loving, capable parents for forced adoption or long term foster care, damaging the children psychologically and emotionally. Local authorities pay independent expert witnesses huge sums of money to write reports based on biased, inaccurate and grossly distorted information. Parents are often accused of being "uncooperative," based on a single informant's view. Parents have no chance once children are removed, lawfully or unlawfully – they instantly become a target for forced adoption. Annabelle committed **suicide** by hanging herself to death days after discovering her baby had been adopted. (The Daily Mail, 6-1-11),

**SUSAN SMITH**. Smith claimed when she committed **suicide** by letting her car roll into a South Carolina lake *with her two sons strapped to their car seats,* she was taking them with her to "protect them." Revenge during a divorce and custody dispute can also provoke maternal filicide, the formal name for such killings. Postpartum mental illness, which can last indefinitely, can range in severity from depression to psychosis to personality disorder, as with mothers who attempt or succeed at committing **suicide** and have "taken the children with them,"

**ANN LENTMER**. Lentmer, a single New York woman who gave birth after fertility treatment, committed **suicide,** leaving behind a baby boy, an estranged lover, and a complex custody case." (Source: Elizabeth Scott, *"The Suicide of Ann Lentmer, "* The Village Voice News, 7-31-13)

**10% of new _Dads_ showed signs of moderate or severe postpartum depression compared to 14% of new Moms.**
(Source: *Journal of Pediatrics,* August 2006)

In the 1940s through the 1970s, unwed fathers were often left out of the adoption decision, were assumed not interested in establishing paternity, and had no legal claim of parental rights, nor was child support enforceable. Even after the 1970s, "Birth" Fathers attracted little notice until 1988 when Jon Ryan organized "National Association of Birthfathers and Reform (NOBAR)," a group of 125 "Birth" Fathers, then headquartered in Baltimore. They told us *"The stereotype of unwed fathers is false and a lot more men are involved in their children's lives than people think. All the search agencies, all the conferences, every single group in the country is reporting more birthfathers coming forward."* Data on how loss of their children to adoption was an unresolved issue and the lack of legal protections were published. (Source: Eva Y. Deykin, PhD, Patricia Patti, MS, and Jon Ryan, BA, in *"Fathers of Adopted Children: A Study of the Impact of Child Surrender on Birthfamilies,"* 3-24-10; and American Journal of Orothopsychiatry, Vol, 58, Issue 2, p 249-248, 1988). Ryan began filing lawsuits in behalf of fathers whose children were relinquished by the mothers without their knowledge and/or under pressure of baby brokers who sent pregnant women to Canada for the birth and adoption of their babies in order to circumvent fathers' parental rights under state laws in the U.S. In the 1980s-1990s, Attorney David Keene Leavitt, a Beverly Hills baby broker, was successfully sued for $8-million for conspiring to help a woman give up her child for adoption *against the father's wishes.* NOBAR and AmFOR intervened, sending mass mailings to U.S. legislators and Canadian courts, objecting to Leavitt's practice of soliciting pregnant women via newspaper ads, nationwide, to come to California, where he was licensed to practice, and where he would then arrange for them to deliver their babies in Canada, making the children Canadian citizens who would then be adopted by Canadians in order to *prevent* the U.S. fathers from asserting their claims of parental rights. Such tactics were utilized because many birthfathers *did* care and *did* want to be fathers to their children. At the time, the number of American children being adopted by foreign parents is a number that wasn't tracked, according to the U.S. Department of State. However, since then, Canadian immigration statistics showed that: 600 U.S. born children had been **adopted** by Canadians since 1995. Experts speculate that the number of children placed abroad is growing. Just one Indianapolis adoption attorney, Steven Kirsh, placed over 100 American-born children since 1991." Baby Broker, Attorney David Leavitt, was successfully sued for $8-million for conspiring to help a woman give up her child for adoption against the father's wishes. (Sources: Paul Dean, *"Birthfathers Are Coming Out of the Shadows,"* Los Angeles Times, quoted in the *Sarasota Herald-Tribune,* 1-30-90; *"The Adoption History Project";* Karen Stabiner, *"The Baby Brokers,"* Los Angeles Times Magazine, 8-14-88; *"The Open Record"* newsletter of Americans For Open Records-AmFOR). Add unintended loss of a child due to divorce or **adoption**, and the numbers are now believed to be far greater than for custodial fathers. The difference between a *custodial* dad who's depressed and a father who has *lost* a child is that the custodial dad may feel fatigued and anxious, is preoccupied with finances, begins to withdraw from the family, is irritable, sleeps poorly or too much, or becomes very angry, may rely on alcohol or other substances for relaxation or escape. Profound changes brought about by caring for the infant are also frequently claimed to cause PPD. PPD is more obvious in fathers who have lost children in divorce custody battles or from unintended or forced **adoption** relinquishments.

**Every year 24,000 men commit suicide.**
**Every 22 minutes one male commits suicide.**
Based on the fact that divorced or separated men are
2-1/2 to 3 times more likely to commit suicide than married men.
A divorced *Father* is 10 times more likely to commit suicide
than a divorced Mother.
15,000 to 18,000 men who commit suicide each year are
most likely *Fathers.*

"Divorced men are often devastated by the loss of their children. It's a little known fact that in the United States men initiate only a small number of the divorces involving children. Most of the men never saw their divorces coming, and they are often treated very unfairly by the family courts." (<u>Sources</u>: *Journal of Epidemiology and Community Health*, Y-2000; CBS News 3-14-00, cbsnews.com/stories/2000/03/14

Perhaps women form greater supportive networks, such as meaningful friendships, at a higher level than men, and regardless of their marital status. So when their marital status changes, women have their friends. (<u>Source</u>: *"Marital Status and Suicide in the National Longitudinal Mortality Study,"* published in the *Journal of Epidemiology and Community Health*, November 2000, which considered data from the *National Longitudinal Mortality Study*, 1979 to 1989 together with U.S. population estimated by U.S. Bureau of the Census.)

*"Families Need Fathers"* has long campaigned for a "presumption of shared parenting in legislation" in Family Courts, and the 2014 Children and Families Act represents a move in the right direction and which may help prevent unnecessary family dismemberment from post-divorce custody decisions and from **adoption**. Along with other supporters of shared parenting though, were some concerns as to whether the application of the law, which was amended a number of times throughout the progress of the Bill, will be carried out in such a way that fewer children will be faced with the prospect of losing contact with a parent where there is no valid reason for this to happen. (<u>Sources</u>: *"Birthfathers: The Forgotten Half of the Story,"* Adoptive Families Magazine, 2001; *"The Baby Brokers,"* Los Angeles Times Magazine, 8-14-88; and The Oregonian, 7-4-04; *"Families Need Fathers"* webpage, April 2014)

# ADOPTEES WHO KILLED

(Serial Killers, Parent Killers, Mass Murderers, School Shooters, and Others whose stories are detailed in "ADOPTED KILLERS," on Amazon)

Abdela, Daphne
Albright, Charles Frederick
    ("*The Eyeball Killer*")
Anderson, Antwan "Twan" D.
Atkins, Joseph
Andrews, Charles D
Baer, Kenneth
Bamber, Jeremy
Barnett, David M.
Barone, Cesar Francesco
Barraza, Juana
    ("*The Old Lady Killer*")
Bartsch, Juergen
Baxter, Henry
Beange, Graham
Beardslee, Donald, 18
Belmonte, Gerard "Gerry"
Benefiel Jr., Bill J.
Bennett Jr, Robert Lee
    ("*Handcuff Man*")
Berkowitz, David
    ("*Son of Sam*")
Bernardo Paul Kenneth
    ("*Ken and Barbi Killers*")
Bessey, Michael
Bianchi, Kenneth Angelo
    ("*Hillside Stranglers*")
Bittaker, Lawrence Sigmund
    ("*The Toolbox Killers*")
Black, Robert
Bluml, Anthony
Bocook, Charles

Bocook, Gladys
Boggess, Clifford Holt
Bonin, William George
    ("*The Freeway Killers*")
Boost, Werner
    ("*Couples Killers*")
Boulet, Matthew
Bourgeois-Greer, Michael
Borden, Lizzie
Bowles, Gary Ray
    ("*The Gay Bar Murders*")
Brady, Ian
    ("*Moors Murders*")
Brewer, Carl Edward
Bridewell, Sandra Camille
    ("*The Black Widow*")
Branch, Margaret Fuss
Bruno, Stephen Joseph
Bruster, Michael
Bundy, Theodore "Ted"
    ("*The Co-ed Killer*")
Buono, Angelo
    ("*Hillside Stranglers*")
Caffrey, Tim
Camerlengo, Thomas
Cameron, Rodney Frances
    ("*Lonely Hearts Killer*")
Campbell, Patrick
Cannon, Joseph John
Carriero, Michael
Carter, Marcus
Carter, Sean

Cassell, Daniel
Catlin, Steven David
Champion, Ryan
Chandler, Vincent "Petey"
Chase, Jeffrey
Chiatti, Luigi
Cipriano, Tucker
Clark, Dilan
Clark Jr., James B.
Clayton, Hugo
Clemons, Jacob S.
Cole, Jaime Piero
Coleman, Alton
Collier, Joseph (Zimmer, Peter)
Collins, John Norman
     ("*Co-ed Killer*")
Conde, Rory
     ("*Tamiani Killer*")
Cooke, Joshua
Corne, James
Cotton, Marcus
Coulson, Robert Otis
Cox, Johnnie Michael
Crawford, Andre
Cruz, Nikolas
     ("*Parkland School Shooter*")
Cunningham, Traci
Dalzell, Andrew
D'Aoust, Heather Marie
Day, Tony
Dean, Jessica
Degelleke, Patrick
Desalvo, Albert
     ("*Boston Strangler*")
Devlin, Michael
Diaz, Monica
DiBenedetto-Heikkila,
     Matthew

Dion, Matthew
Dowdell, Richard
Dreyer, Henry Lee
Duff-Smith, Markum
Dugas, Gaetan
     ("*Patient Zero*")
Du Plooy, Schalk
Dye, Cameron
Dye, Garrett
Eastlack, John Patrick
Eyeler, Larry
     ("*Interstate Killer*")
Fears, Randall Alan
Freund, William
     ("*The Terror Campaign*")
Foell, David
Ford, Patrick Hunter
Forman, Joseph
Frazier, Ryan James
Fuss, Charles Allen
Fuss Able Erives, Melissa
Fyfe, William Patrick
     ("*The Plumber*")
Gallo, Travis
Garner, Joseph
Gebauer, John Frank
George, Brad
Georges, Guy
     ("*Beast of the Bastile*")
Gerlach, Clayton
Geronimo, Roderick
Gilmore, Gary Mark
Goodman, Sierra,
Goodman, Spencer Corey
Goswick, Joseph Wayne Cook
Graham, Harrison T "Marty"
     ("*Cookie Monster Killer*")
Grant, Matthew,

Graves, Jennifer Irene,
Gray, Dana Sue,
Gray, Dorothea Helen (Puente)
Gufler, Max
Gunning, James
Hagen, Marjorie Caldwell
Hale, Bill
     *("Osage Killer")*
Hall, Edwin Ray
Hall, Gabriel
Hamilton, Thomas
     *("Dunblane School Shooter")*
Hamlin, Boy,
Hargon, Ernest Lee,
Harper Jr., Edward, "Eddie" Lee
Harr, Bryan Andrew
Harries, Thomas Ronald Lewis
Harvey, Holly
Hatley, Hershal
Hauser, Daniel Patrick
Hawkins, Robert A.
     *("Westroads Mall Shooter")*
Heater, Naomi Kimberly
Hedlund, Charles Michael
Heavy Runner, Mark St. Storm
Helder, Lucas "Luke" John
     *("Smiley Face Mail Bomber")*
Helm, Roger Scott
Hendricks, Billy Lynn
Hirko, Kim
Hittle, Daniel Joe
Hoadley, Darrell
Holmes, James Egan
Hoskins, Robert
Howard, Aaron
Hungerford, Brandi Lynn
Hyde, Ronnie Leon
James, Boy

Jenkins, Joshua Bradley
Jett, Jacob
Johnson, Lamont S.
Jones, James
Jones, Timothy Jason
Jordan, Johnnie
Kallinger, Joseph
     *("Philadelphia Shoemaker")*
Kamin, Moses
Kasten, Daniel
Katz, David
Kelsall, Daniel "Jack"
     *("The Lover")*
Kimble, Paul
Kimes, Sante
King, John William
Kipp, Martin James
     *("Dr. Crazy")*
Kipapa, K'Ano'i
Kirby, Christopher
Kislov, Yaroslav
Knoller, Marjorie,
Knowles, Paul John
     *("Casanova Killer")*
Knight, Julian
Komisarjevsky, Joshua A.
Knoefel, Kevin
Kondro, Joseph Robert
     *("The 'Uncle Joe' Killer")*
Koslow, Kristi
Krajcir, Timothy Wayne
Krebs, Rex Allan
Kredrowitz, Nikalas
Kreutzer, Paul W.
La Loche School Shooter
Lacey, Terrell L.
LaGrand, Karl
LaGrand, Walter

Lai, Chuni
Lajos, Domingo
Lake, Starr M.
Lane, Thomas "T.J."
    *("Ohio School Shooter")*
Lang, Scott
Lanier, Boy
Lee, Bruce George Peter
Lee, Eric
Lee, John
Legrand, Michael
Linares, Desire
Lindh, Aaron
Lindquist, Matthew
Lishing, Elijah D.
Little Jr., Charlie
Little, Samuel
Long, Justin Ryan
Longo, Christian, Preston
Lonneberg-Lane
Lopez, Pedro Alonzo
    *("Monster of the Andes")*
Losicco, Richard
Losicco, Terrence
Lovgren, John Ingvar
MacDonald, Gabriel
MacDonald, Grace
Magliolo, Michael Scott
Magnotta, Luka
Malvo, Lee Boyd
    *("The Beltway Snipers")*
Mann, Warlito
Marcus, Aaron
Marin-Doan, Jordan
Marks, Taylor Melissa Mary
Martinez, Alexander Ray
McCourt, David
McCray, Alvario Samell

McElrath, Damien
McKnight, Robert
McMath, James
McMullen, Jonathan
Menard, Brandon Christopher
Miller, Dewayne
Miller, George
Mitchell, Royce
Monks, Christopher
Montgomery, Lisa,
Moorman, Robert Henry
Mox, Gregory Richard
Muhammad, Rehman
Mullis, Travis
Mulzac, Jayvon
Munro, James Michael
    *("The Freeway Killers")*
Nelson, Eric Leonard
Ngoma, Wakhile
Niedere, Mathew
Niiranen, Patrick
Norris, Roy
    *("The Toolbox Killers")*
O'Connell, Brenda
O'Connell, Catherine
O'Driscoll, Jonathan
Oken, Steven
Ogorzow, Paul
Onoprienko, Anatoly Yaiyvych
Ortiz, Jeffrey Richard
Parker, Gabriel
Pagnam, Brian E.
Pang, Martin
Payne, Eric
Pelley, Robert Jeffrey
Perry, Michael James
Peterson, Angel
Peterson, Seth Gordon

Phillips Jr., Frederick O.
Pierce, Darci
Pilato, Michael
Pine, Zachariah E.
Pinkleton, Walker Wayne
Pitts, Shayne J.
Pollard, Michel
Posey, Cody
Povich, Holly,
Pribbernow, Steven Jeffrey
Prink, Timothy
Purdy, Patrick Edward
    *("Cleveland School Massacre")*
Ramos, Marcelino
Ray, Justin
Regan, Mark
Rendell, Elena Janelle
Reese, John Loveman
Reeves, Randolph
Reynolds, Irene
Reynolds, Jaquiline "Nikki"
Rice, Jr., Michael Joe
Richards Jr., Luther Charles
Richardson, Christopher A,
Rifkin, Joel
Riley, Matthew
Robison, Boy
Rodrigues, Ricky
Rogers, Anthony L.
Rogers, Dayton Leroy
    *("Molalla Forest Killer")*
Ross, Johnny
Rung, Thomas "Pinocchio"
Sachs, Ashton
Saldivar, Dakota
Saunders, Peter
Savin, Ionut Silviu
Sawdon, John

Schmid, Charles Howard"Smitty"
    *("Pied Piper of Tucson")*
Scott, Darryl
Sellers, Sean Richard
Sells, Tommy Lynn
Share, Catherine Gypsy
    *("Manson Family")*
Shaughnessy, Nicolas
Shawcross, Arthur J.
Shellman, James
Sherman, Timothy Scott
Shields, Alexis
Sikorski, Roksana
Singleton, James Joseph
Sithole, Moses
Skalitzky Matthew
Skinner, Tia Marie Mitchell
Skocz, Jeremy
"SLD"
Smith, Eric
Smullen, Bruno Lorenzo
Snell, James M.
Sobhraj, Charles
    *("The Bikini Killer")*
Soni, Gita
Spangler, Robert Merlin
    *("Black Widower")*
Spearman, Josh
Speck, Richard
Stano, Gerald Eugene
Stein, Steven
Steinlicht, Mark Ernie
Steinman, Garry
Stevenson, Galen
Stewart, Gary L.
Stoddard, Daniel Paul
Stuart, Tashia
Struebing, Kurt Alan

Stuber, Joseph Andrew
Sturgel, Timothy
Stutzman, Rodney R.
Sutton, Christopher
Swartz, Larry
Swartz, Michael
Sweet, Isaiah R.
Swofford, Jerry
Tankleff, Marty M. "Marty"
Taylor, Kaleb David
Terhune, Cameron Richard
Testo, Jonathan
Thomas, Douglas Christopher
Thomas, Nigel
Thomasson, Bradley Ryan
Thornburn, Trent
Thornton, Jamie Grant
Tomassoni, Kathryn Marie
Tomassoni, Tammie Marie
Tombs, Jennifer
Toppan, Jane
        ("*Angel of Death*")
Toole, Otis Edward
Triplett, Marvin Matthew
Troiano, James
"Jimmie"Anthony
Tucson boy
Turner Carlton Akee
U.K. Adoptee
Unterweger, Johann "Jack"
        ("*Vienna Strangler*")
Van Duyne, Arnell
Van Dyken Fred Daniel
        ("*Long Soldier*")
Van Strum, Jordan
Vidinhar, Aza Ray
Villareal, Juan Alberto
Vinod, Girl

Wade, Susan Ellen
Waldon, Billy Ray
Wallace, Marcus
Watts, Carl "Coral" Eugene
        ("*Sunday Morning Slasher*")
Weaver, Keith Chul
Weightman, David
Weise, Jeff
        ("*Red Lake School Shooter*")
Welche, Lee Roy
White, Miriam
Whitehead, Jasmiyah ("Jas")
Whitehead, Tasmiyah ("Tas")
Whitehead, K
Whitlow, Antonio
Wheeler, Codee
Wilken, Stewart,
Williams, Tavares Eugene
Wilson, Michael
Wolmarans, Frederik
Wood, Boy
Woodard-Hebert, Boy
Woodcock, Peter
        (David Michael Kreuger)
Woodham, Luke Timms
Woodruff, David Wayne
Wuornos, Aileen Carol Pitman
        ("*Damsel of Death*")
Worley, Ron
Wright,Mitchell
Yates, Robert Lee
        ("*Spokane Serial Killer*")
Yesconis, Jennifer Nicole
Young, Graham Frederick
        ("*Teacup Poisoner*")
Young, Mikhail
Yuskoff, Joe
Zimmer,Peter (JosephCollier)
Zunich, Sabrina

# The Guardian

## A 'hellish world': the mental health crisis overwhelming America's prisons

In America, jails and prisons have become the nation's de facto mental healthcare providers - and the results are chilling

In *One Flew Over the Cuckoo's Nest*, Ken Kesey describes two kinds of patients in the psychiatric hospital where the story is set: Acutes ("because the doctors figure them still sick enough to be fixed") and Chronics (who are "in for good, the staff concedes").

When Kristopher Rodriguez, a 31-year-old man from Florida, first went into the US criminal justice system in 2008, it seemed like he would have been classified as an Acute; now nearly a decade later, he would almost certainly qualify as a Chronic.

A tall, strapping boy whose friends called him Dino, as in "dinosaur", Rodriguez was diagnosed with schizophrenia when he was around 14. His mother, Gemma Pena, had come home from work one night to find that he had disconnected the hot water heater, convinced that the CIA was using it to spy on him.

At first she thought his behavior was simply evidence of grief over his grandmother's death a few months earlier; Rodriguez had been especially close to her. But when he continued to act strangely, saying he was hearing voices, Pena called the police and had him hospitalized against his will.

It was the first of perhaps a dozen times that she had him "Baker Acted", as it is known in Florida - after the 1971 law governing involuntary hospitalizations. The next few years were a blur of doctors appointments, drug use, homelessness, arrests and voluntary and involuntary hospitalizations.

Rodriguez is currently serving a 10-year sentence in a Florida state prison for trying to rob somebody at gunpoint when he was 22. He spent five years in jail before he took the plea bargain; people with mental illness often spend far longer in jail waiting for their cases to be resolved.

During his time in jail, he was sick enough that he had to be hospitalized three separate times - twice for psychiatric crises and once because he was so psychotic that he

97

mutilated his genitals. His mother said the second psychiatric hospitalization was the last time she saw him lucid.

Nevertheless, after he accepted a plea bargain, Rodriguez was transferred to prison. His first few months there, he lived in general population. (One wonders how Florida's department of corrections was not notified of the extent of his illness before he arrived.) After a few months of occasional run-ins with prison staff, he was moved to a unit for prisoners with mental illness.

About a year ago, his condition deteriorated to such an extent that he was moved to the Lake Correctional Institution, a prison north-west of Orlando that is equipped with an inpatient psychiatric unit.

Even so, his mother says, her son remains severely psychotic, an assessment apparently shared by the Florida department of corrections, which regularly denies Pena visits on the basis that Rodriguez is too sick to see her.

**More than 50 years** after Kesey's novel, state psychiatric hospitals of the sort he described are, like lobotomies, long gone. Yet if we think that the hellish world Kesey captured belongs to another era, we are deluded.

It's true that the *hospitals* have mostly disappeared: between 1950 and 2000 the number of people with serious mental illness living in psychiatric institutions dropped from almost half a million people to about 50,000. But none of the rest of it has gone away, not the cruelty, the filth, the bad food or the brutality. Nor, most importantly, has the large population of people with mental illness, like Rodriguez, who are kept largely out of sight, their poor treatment invisible to most ordinary Americans.

The only real difference between Kesey's time and our own is that the mistreatment of people with mental illness now happens in jails and prisons. Today, the country's largest providers of psychiatric care are not hospitals at all, but rather the jails in Chicago, Los Angeles and New York City.

Across the country, correctional facilities are struggling with the reality that they have become the nation's de facto mental healthcare providers, although they are hopelessly ill-equipped for the job. They are now contending with tens of thousands of people with mental illness who, by some counts, make up as much as half of their populations.

Little acknowledged in public debate, this situation is readily apparent in almost every correctional facility in the country. In Michigan, roughly half of all people in county jails have a mental illness, and nearly a quarter of people in state prisons do. In 2016, the state spent nearly $4m on psychiatric medication for state prisoners. In Iowa about a third of people in prison have a serious mental illness; another quarter have a chronic mental health diagnosis.

Meanwhile, nearly half of the people executed nationwide between 2000 and 2015 had been diagnosed with a mental illness and/or substance use disorder in their adult lives.

When a legal settlement required California to build a psychiatric unit on its death row at San Quentin the 40 beds were filled immediately.

The mental health crisis is especially pronounced among women prisoners: one study by the US Bureau of Justice Statistics found that 75% of women incarcerated in jails and prisons had a mental illness, as compared with just over 60% and 55% of men, respectively. A more recent study showed that 20% of women in jail and 30% in prison had experienced "serious psychological distress" in the month before the survey, compared with 14% and 26% of men, respectively.

Although the overall number of people behind bars in the US has decreased in recent years, the proportion of prisoners with mental illness has continued to go up. In 2010, about 30% of people at New York's Rikers Island jail had a mental illness; in 2014, the figure rose to 40% , and by 2017, it had gone up to 43%. Studies of the most frequently arrested people in New York, Los Angeles and elsewhere have found that they are far more likely than others to have mental illness, to require antipsychotic medications while incarcerated and to have a substance use problem.

That there are so many people with mental illness locked in our jails and prisons is but one piece of the crisis. Along with race and poverty, mental illness has become a salient feature of mass incarceration, one that must be accounted for in any discussion about criminal justice reform.

Mental illness affects every aspect of the criminal justice system, from policing to the courts to prisons and beyond. Nor are the effects limited to the criminal justice system; many people with mental illness cycle back and forth between jail or prison and living in the community.

The racial inequity of the criminal justice system has been widely noted: it is estimated that one out of every three African American men and one of every six Hispanic men born in 2001 will be arrested in their lifetimes.

But for Americans with serious mental illness, it is estimated that as many as one in two will be arrested at some point in their lives. It's not just arrests. One in four of the nearly 1,000 fatal police shootings in 2016 involved a person with mental illness, according to a study by the Washington Post. The Post estimated that mental illness was a factor in a quarter of fatal police shootings in 2017, too.

People with mental illness are among the most disadvantaged members of our society, and when they end up in the criminal justice system, they tend to fare worse than others. People with mental illness are less likely to make bail and more likely to face longer sentences. They are more likely to end up in solitary confinement, less likely to make parole and more likely to commit suicide.

Yet jail and prison have become, for many people, their primary means of getting mental healthcare. Their experiences offer an especially eye-opening view of a criminal justice system that today houses more than two million people and costs us hundreds of billions of dollars a year.

**Gemma Pena says** that she writes her son regularly but that it's been years since Kristopher has written back. She sent him pictures of herself and his brothers and niece but he tore them up.

When she does get to visit him, the son who used to take pride in being a natty dresser smells terrible and is often visibly dirty, as if he hasn't bathed in weeks, even though sh regularly puts money into his commissary account so that he can buy toiletries. (Prisoners who want basic items, from potato chips to a radio to toothpaste and shampoo, have to use the money in their commissary accounts, usually provided by family and friends.)

During their last visit he got so agitated, yelling and pounding his fists on the table, that the corrections officers handcuffed and shackled him, and took him away strapped into a wheelchair. His medical records show that his medication compliance has been spotty sometimes Rodriguez refuses to take it, and other times it hasn't been available becaus the supplier didn't deliver it to the prison.

For years now, Rodriguez has been stuck in this sad limbo: according to the state, he is well enough to stay incarcerated, but far too sick to live in the general prison population or even to get regular visits from his mother.

Lawyers who have examined his case say his story is typical. Florida's prisons have bee the subject of repeated investigations for their treatment of prisoners with mental illness; so have jails and prisons in other states, including California, Illinois and Alabama.

The investigations are critical, as are the changes to policy and protocol that they can produce. But jails and prisons are filled with thousands of people like Kristopher Rodriguez. And as long as we continue to lock them up, the problem is going to keep getting worse.

*Adapted from Insane: America's Criminal Treatment of Mental Illness. Copyright © 2018 by Alisa Roth. Available from Basic Books, an imprint of Perseus Books, a division of PBG Publishing, LLC, a subsidiary of Hachette Book Group, Inc*

# The Prison System Is Designed to Ignore Mental Illness

**Negligence, delays in diagnosis, and flat-out abuse are rampant.**

By Maggie Puniewska  |  Jun 1 2017, 10:00am

In 2005, Deneise Younger went to prison for forging nearly a whole checkbook's worth of checks after a former partner slighted her. A few months into her sentence, she lost her temper with another inmate and placed razor blades in her shoes. For that, she was sent to solitary confinement for 180 days and her sentence was extended another year. While Younger had several of these impulsive reactions in her life, it wasn't until three months into her time in the South Carolina prison system that she was diagnosed with intermittent explosive disorder and manic depression. "I never realized what it was," Younger, 36, told me over the phone. "You just get real angry and without thinking, you act, not knowing that you have reacted or said something stupid until after the fact. When I was putting those razor blades in her shoes, I knew what I was doing, but not in the moment, and afterward I felt so bad. Like, 'Why did I just do that?'"

While Younger was able to reflect on her offenses in solitary confinement, the punishment made it difficult to manage her anger and depression. "I was so mad in there. I would beat the door, I would scream and cry. It was awful. I felt

101

worthless, I felt helpless, I felt lost. I was embarrassed," she says. Aside from the psychiatric medication that was dropped off at her cell door once daily after her diagnosis, she didn't have access to any sort of mental health counseling that could help her make sense of her newly identified conditions.

**In some instances, guards, officers, physicians, and inmates themselves were unaware that they had a condition like PTSD or a personality disorder for more than two years.**

"I only saw the psychiatrist once a month to review how my medication was going, but I would have wanted someone to talk to a little bit more often," she says. "You are already angry, you are already grieving being in prison with all the rules and different personalities and the neglect, it's better when you can talk to someone and express yourself, you know?"

Without anyone to help her cope, Younger ended up in solitary with another impulsive episode and landed on suicide watch for seven days, even though she didn't have any suicidal thoughts or intentions. While this meant that she was checked in on more frequently, again, she didn't receive any sort of mental health counseling during or after the incident.

Unfortunately, Younger's case isn't an outlier. According to the last report by the **Bureau of Justice Statistics**, nearly 50 percent of US inmates have mental health conditions but only 34 percent of state prison inmates had professional mental health therapy after being admitted to prison; the number is even lower for those in local jails, just 18 percent. So, thousands of individuals had, and undoubtedly have, to navigate America's meager mental health services in correctional facilities. What are they up against? Delayed diagnoses, ineffective and often abusive care, and violence. But denying mental health care, whether intentionally or not, to individuals doing time isn't just unconstitutional, it can create bigger problems down the line: declining mental health, extended sentences, and increased risk of recidivism.

The trouble can start as soon as someone with a mental health condition enters a correctional facility. Like Younger, many inmates receive their first mental health diagnosis in prison, but it isn't right away. In a new study published in April, researchers combed through records of more than 8500 Iowa state prison inmates and found that a whopping 99 percent of mental health diagnoses were first made during incarceration, some as late as 29 months into a prisoner's sentence. That means that in some instances, guards, officers, physicians, and inmates themselves were unaware that they had a condition like PTSD or a personality disorder for more than two years.

Diagnosing mental illness is undeniably difficult in many circumstances, but the way mental health care is currently run in American correctional facilities seems to make it extra challenging to figure out who needs help. For starters, confidential disclosure can be nearly impossible. Michael Bien, a San Francisco-based attorney who successfully sued the state of California for its overcrowded prisons, represents inmates with physical and psychological disabilities and has heard numerous complaints about discretion.

"A lot of prisoners have told me that when they finally got the courage to ask the guards to see a mental health professional, there wasn't any confidential space to do so," he says. "Instead, someone will come over to your cell and talk to you through the cell door. It's loud and everyone can hear you—why *would you* tell someone you are hearing voices or have thought about killing yourself? It can be completely embarrassing, especially in prison, where there's an expectation to be tough." It may be the reason some inmates are choosing to stay silent, and only get noticed once their condition worsens and they act out.

Delayed diagnosis can also be a part of behavioral issues. "People who are diagnosed late or not at all may act out, become violent, or create problems for themselves or other prisoners," says Tala Al-Rousan, a research fellow at Harvard's School of Public Health who was the lead author on the Iowa state prison study. "These behavioral problems can result in sentences being extended to make it extra challenging to figure out who needs help. For starters, confidential disclosure can be nearly impossible. Michael Bien, a San Francisco-based attorney who successfully sued the state of California for its overcrowded prisons, represents inmates with physical and psychological disabilities and has heard numerous complaints about discretion.

"A lot of prisoners have told me that when they finally got the courage to ask the guards to see a mental health professional, there wasn't any confidential space to do so," he says. "Instead, someone will come over to your cell and talk to you through the cell door. It's loud and everyone can hear you — why *would you* tell someone you are hearing voices or have thought about killing yourself? It can be completely embarrassing, especially in prison, where there's an expectation to be tough." It may be the reason some inmates are choosing to stay silent, and only get noticed once their condition worsens and they act out.

Delayed diagnosis can also be a part of behavioral issues. "People who are diagnosed late or not at all may act out, become violent, or create problems for themselves or other prisoners," says Tala Al-Rousan, a research fellow at Harvard's School of Public Health who was the lead author on the Iowa state prison study. "These behavioral problems can result in sentences being extended or harsh punishment like solitary confinement that can worsen their condition, leading to more behavioral issues—it's a cycle that can go on for years."

In federal prison, 40 percent of inmates with mental health conditions were charged with rule violations like physical assault, compared to about 28 percent that didn't have them, according to the Bureau of Justice Statistics report above. It doesn't mean that people with psychiatric conditions are necessarily more prone to violence, Al-Rousan says, but it may be that the difficulty of managing symptoms with negligent care and the stressful prison environment contribute to acting out—that connection is still being studied, she adds.

**Watch More on VICE:** Meet One of Britain's Most Notorious Reformed Criminals

Lack of staffing—another pervasive issue that heavily contributes to the grim state of mental health services—may mean that mental health professionals only have time for group therapy instead of individual meetings, an arrangement that can force people to clam up. "After we got court orders for California prisons to do group therapy, we learned that some of the sessions were not effective," Bien says. "The sessions wouldn't be tailored to one condition and every time people showed up, there would be different inmates in the group. The whole point of a group is that you are developing relationships and trust with those people. If it's different people every time, you're not going to want to talk about what's really on your mind, especially in prison where you are already worried about confidentiality."

**Do we want them to be functional, productive people who are able to hold a job or do we want them to be so disabled by mental illness that they can't function?**

Several investigations that have dug into the matter have uncovered shocking and unconstitutional levels of care in prisons and jails. In 2014, the Southern Poverty Law Center (SPLC) and the Alabama Disabilities Advocacy Program filed a lawsuit **suing the Alabama Department of Corrections** for "grossly inadequate" medical and mental health care that "subjects all prisoners to a substantial risk of serious harm, including unnecessary pain, loss of function, injury and death."

Maria Morris, a SPLC attorney who developed the lawsuit, spent three years interviewing inmates and pouring over medical records and contracts with a team of experts before filing it. She recounted some of the grievances to me, many of which expose why early diagnosis and effective treatment aren't happening. For example, nurses without any mental health reported being medicated against their will and were sent to solitary confinement until they would agree to take medication; many have never received a hearing to determine if it's necessary to take medication in the first place. Inmates on suicide watch would be left alone for days at a time—ironically, no one was watching them.

Mentally ill inmates can find themselves in solitary confinement, also called segregation, which is more often a placement that can aggravate their condition. In 2014, the American Civil Liberties Union (ACLU) and the Prison Law Office sued the Arizona Department of Corrections for excessive use of solitary confinement, among other things. "Prisoners with mental health issues in Arizona aren't being adequately treated, so they are accumulating disciplinary charges, which if you have enough, you will work your way into solitary confinement," says David Fathi, director of the National Prison Project at the ACLU, who argued the case for prisoners in the Court of Appeals for the Ninth Circuit.

"But it's completely uncontroversial that solitary confinement exacerbates preexisting mental illness and impacts the suicide rate, so it's really a lethal combination." An analysis of inmates in New York City jails found that more

108

education—"essentially like the ones who take your blood pressure at the doctor's office," Morris said—would determine whether an Alabama inmate needed to see a psychiatrist. Without any psychiatric training, how would they know who qualified?

In many instances, inmates saw unlicensed counselors who were technically not supposed to be practicing without close supervision. Therapy sessions sometimes lasted for just five to ten minutes, and occurred weeks apart, even for patients who were severely ill with disorders like schizophrenia. One of her clients, who Morris referred to as "among the sickest people in the system," was locked in his cell for more than 23 hours a day and received all of his "counseling sessions" by essentially shouting through a solid metal door. (The Alabama Department of Corrections did not respond to a request for comment on this.)

S ubpar care is only one part of the grim reality of being in prison with a mental health condition. Sadly, many mentally ill inmates are also often abused and denied care, even when it's clear that they are suffering. During interviews with inmates, Morris and her team learned of too many situations that fell into that category. One inmate cut himself on five separate occasions but never received mental health care. Numerous prisoners than **50 percent of self-harm occurred** in **solitary confinement** and another study found that its associated with an **increased risk for PTSD** upon release.

Morris also told me about instances where mental health symptoms were confused with acting out. A client of hers that was schizophrenic was responding to voices in his head instead of following guards' orders. He was beat up by them and placed into segregation for lack of compliance. "Sometimes people are definitely put into segregation because they have done something violent which may or may not be related to a mental health problem...but there are also people who get placed into segregation in Alabama for essentially being hard to manage and I think certainly a lot of those individual are individuals with mental health problems. Unfortunately, mentally ill people are more susceptible to the harms of segregation, than people who aren't mentally ill," Morris said.

One of the most difficult things to hear Younger recall was the physical and verbal abuse directed toward mentally ill inmates, including herself. "There were some guards that would just do picky things to spite you, like turn off the TV early or threaten to put you in lockdown," she says. "There was one time where they harassed a woman who had some real bad issues. This one particular guard took her cigarette and told her she wasn't getting any more. She was trying to get the cigarette back and they maced her, hit her with the radio, and the other guards handcuffed her. Blood was everywhere. I went through a lot of emotions seeing something like that: I was angry, I was scared, I cried. If you could do something like that to someone who really really really didn't do anything, what would you do to me?"

According to a 2015 report by Human Rights Watch, "corrections officials at times needlessly and punitively deluge [prisoners with mental disabilities] with chemical sprays; shock them with electric stun devices; strap them to chairs and beds for days on end; break their jaws, noses, ribs; or leave them with lacerations, second degree burns, deep bruises, and damaged internal organs. The violence can traumatize already vulnerable men and women, aggravating their symptoms and making future mental health treatment more difficult."

"There is a very serious problem with a lack of accountability in regards to what [prison staff] can do," Morris says. "And I think when you add someone who is seriously mentally ill to the mix, the lack of accountability becomes even greater because those prisoners have a hard time getting people to believe what they are experiencing in prison...the men who are severely mentally ill in Alabama seem to be particularly vulnerable to violence by the guards."

In order to begin to repair the broken mental health system, it's clear that prisons desperately need to hire more professionals, and more qualified ones. According to Morris, the Alabama Department of Corrections maintained that their conditions were largely related to dried up funding. "It essentially boiled down to 'We are doing the best we can. We don't have any money, we can't hire more people, we can't hire more psychiatrists because there aren't any more in Alabama,'" she says. "And that's probably true. It's hard to hire for this position because it's a difficult work environment without good pay."

If facilities can only make do with the workforce they have, additional training for both medical staff and officers could lead to better outcomes for inmates. "These are very difficult situations for psychiatrists to navigate and we are presumably as well-trained as anybody to take care of mental illness," says Elizabeth Ford, a psychiatrist who runs New York City's Correctional Health's psychiatric services and oversees mental health care at Rikers Island. "Yet most patients are in settings where most of the staff aren't trained anywhere close to that and are being asked to manage some of the same things. A lot of New York City jails are trying to change that and train staff as best as they can."

When resources are tight, prisons could turn to other, relatively obvious networks for clues on an inmate's mental health. "It would be helpful to get information from an inmate's former provider or a clinic in the community there they were receiving care," Ford says. "But it can be challenging because there's this idea that once someone enters the criminal justice system, you shouldn't be sharing information back and forth with the community. That's enormously challenging." When Al-Rousan spoke with prison psychiatrists in Iowa, they echoed that having access to patient records would enormously help with diagnosis.

Perhaps one of the reasons why mental health care isn't a priority in correctional facilities goes back to the unfavorable attitude that society possesses toward inmates. "Right now a lot of people have the perception that the people in prison should be punished since they are criminals," Fathi says, adding that there's a need for a cultural shift that recognizes the importance of humane and responsible care. "But under the US Constitution, prisons and jails have to provide mental and medical health services that comply with the 8th Amendment — no cruel or unusual punishment. Most prisoners are eventually going to get out and they are going to live down the street from you and me. Do we want them to be functional, productive people who are able to hold a job or do we want them to be so disabled by mental illness that they can't function?"

Morris added, "When we sentence someone to prison, we are taking away a lot. There is no question that if you go to prison, you are being punished. It's loud, it's smelly, and you have no freedom to do much of anything. You don't have the ability to talk to people you love or to touch the people you love — you lose a lot.

But to make someone who is ill suffer from that illness as a punishment is just inhumane. They didn't want this condition, they didn't create it, and they have to be punished more as a result of it? It doesn't seem right—it just seems cruel."

# Autism spectrum

**Autism spectrum**, also known as **autism spectrum disorder (ASD)** or **autism spectrum condition (ASC)**, is a range of neurodevelopmental disorders that includes autism and related conditions. Individuals on the spectrum present with two types of symptoms: problems in social communication and social interaction, and restricted, repetitive patterns of behavior, interests or activities. Symptoms are typically recognized between one and two years of age.[2] Long term issues may include difficulties in creating and keeping relationships, maintaining a job, and performing daily tasks.[8]

The cause of autism spectrum is uncertain.[4] Risk factors include having an older parent, a family history of the condition, and certain genetic conditions.[4] Diagnosis is based on symptoms.[4] The DSM-5 redefined the autism spectrum disorders to encompass the previous diagnoses of autism, Asperger syndrome, pervasive developmental disorder not otherwise specified (PDD-NOS), and childhood disintegrative disorder.[9]

Treatment efforts are generally individualized to the person's condition.[4] Medications may be used to try to help improve certain associated problems.[4] Evidence to support the use of medications, however, is not very strong.[6] Autism spectrum is estimated to affect about 1% of people (62.2 million globally as of 2015).[2][7] Males are diagnosed more often than females.[8]

## Contents

### Autism spectrum

Repetitively stacking or lining up objects is associated with autism.

| | |
|---|---|
| Synonyms | Autism spectrum disorder (ASD), autism spectrum condition (ASC)[1] |
| Specialty | Psychiatry |
| Symptoms | Problems with social communication and social interaction, restricted interests and repetitive behavior[2] |
| Usual onset | By the age of 3 years[3] |
| Risk factors | Advanced parental age, exposure to valproate during pregnancy, low birth weight[2] |
| Diagnostic method | Based on symptoms[4] |
| Differential diagnosis | Intellectual disability, Rett syndrome, ADHD, selective mutism, childhood-onset schizophrenia[2] |
| Treatment | Behavioral therapy,[5] psychotropic medication[6] |
| Medication | Antipsychotics, antidepressants, and psychostimulants (associated symptoms) |
| Frequency | 1% of people[2] (62.2 million 2015)[7] |

## Classification

In the United States, a revision to autism spectrum disorder (ASD) was presented in the *Diagnostic and Statistical Manual of Mental Disorders* version 5 (DSM-5), released May 2013.[10] The new diagnosis encompasses previous diagnoses of autistic disorder, Asperger syndrome, childhood disintegrative disorder, and PDD-NOS. Compared with the DSM-IV diagnosis of autistic disorder, the DSM-5 diagnosis of ASD no longer includes communication as a separate criterion, and has merged social interaction and communication into one category.[11] Slightly different diagnostic definitions are used in other countries. For example, the ICD-10 is the most commonly-used diagnostic manual in the UK and European Union.[12] Rather than categorizing these diagnoses, the DSM-5 has adopted a dimensional approach to diagnosing disorders that fall underneath the autism spectrum umbrella. Some have proposed that individuals on the autism spectrum may be better represented as a single diagnostic category. Within this category, the DSM-5 has proposed a framework of differentiating each individual by dimensions of severity, as well as associated features (i.e., known genetic disorders, and intellectual disability).

Another change to the DSM includes collapsing social and communication deficits into one domain. Thus, an individual with an ASD diagnosis will be described in terms of severity of social communication symptoms, severity of fixated or restricted behaviors or interests, and associated features. The restricting of onset age has also been loosened from 3 years of age to "early developmental period", with a note that symptoms may manifest later when social demands exceed capabilities.[13]

Autism forms the core of the autism spectrum disorders. Asperger syndrome is closest to autism in signs and likely causes;[14] unlike autism, people with Asperger syndrome usually have no significant delay in language development, according to the older DSM-4 criteria.[15] PDD-NOS is diagnosed when the criteria are not met for a more specific disorder. Some sources also include Rett syndrome and childhood disintegrative disorder, which share several signs with autism but may have unrelated causes; other sources differentiate them from ASD, but group all of the above conditions into the pervasive developmental disorders.[14][16]

Autism, Asperger syndrome, and PDD-NOS are sometimes called the *autistic disorders* instead of ASD,[17] whereas autism itself is often called *autistic disorder*, *childhood autism*, or *infantile autism*.[18] Although the older term *pervasive developmental disorder* and the newer term *autism spectrum disorder* largely or entirely overlap,[16] the earlier was intended to describe a specific set of diagnostic labels, whereas the latter refers to a postulated *spectrum disorder* linking various conditions.[19] ASD is a subset of the broader autism phenotype (BAP), which describes individuals who may not have ASD but do have autistic-like traits, such as avoiding eye contact.[18]

# Characteristics

Under the DSM-5, autism is characterized by persistent deficits in social communication and interaction across multiple contexts, as well as restricted, repetitive patterns of behavior, interests, or activities. These deficits are present in early childhood, and lead to clinically significant functional impairment.[20] There is also a unique form of autism called autistic savantism, where a child can display outstanding skills in music, art, and numbers with no practice.[21] Because of its relevance to different populations, self-injurious behaviors (SIB) are not considered a core characteristic of the ASD population however approximately 50% of those with ASD take part in some type of SIB (head-banging, self-biting) and are more at risk than other groups with developmental disabilities.[22]

Other characteristics of ASD include restricted and repetitive behaviors (RRBs) which include a large range of specific gestures and acts, it can even include certain behavioral traits as defined in the Diagnostic and Statistic Manual for Mental Disorders.[23]

Asperger syndrome was distinguished from autism in the DSM-IV by the lack of delay or deviance in early language development.[24] Additionally, individuals diagnosed with Asperger syndrome did not have significant cognitive delays.[25] PDD-NOS was considered "subthreshold autism" and "atypical autism" because it was often characterized by milder symptoms of autism or symptoms in only one domain (such as social difficulties).[26] The DSM-5 eliminated the four separate diagnoses: Asperger Syndrome, Pervasive Developmental Disorder Not Otherwise Specified (PDD-NOS), Childhood Disintegrative Disorder, and Autistic Disorder and combined them under the diagnosis of Autism Spectrum Disorder.[20]

### Behavioral characteristics

Autism spectrum disorders include a wide variety of characteristics that display to a medical professional that a person has this disorder. Some of these include behavioral characteristics which widely range from slow development of social and learning skills to difficulties creating connections with the people around them. They may develop these difficulties of creating connections due to anxiety or depression which people with autism are more prone to having, and as a result isolate themselves.[27] Other behavioral characteristics include abnormal responses to sensations which includes, but is not limited to, sights, sounds, touch, and smell, and problems keeping the rhythm of speech. The problem with keeping the rhythm of speech plays influence on the social skills a person has, as they may not be as easily understood by their communication partner. The behavioral characteristics displayed by those with autism spectrum disorder typically influence development, language, and social competence. Behavioral characteristics of those with autism spectrum disorder can be seen as perceptual disturbances, disturbances of development rate, relating, speech and language, and motility.[28]

### Developmental course

Autism spectrum disorders are thought to follow two possible developmental courses, although most parents report that symptom onset occurred within the first year of life.[29][30] One course of development is more gradual in nature, in which parents report concerns in development over the first two years of life and diagnosis is made around 3–4 years of age. Some of the early signs of ASDs in this course include decreased looking at faces, failure to turn when name is called, failure to show interests by showing or pointing, and delayed pretend play.[31]

A second course of development is characterized by normal or near-normal development followed by loss of skills or regression in the first 2–3 years. Regression may occur in a variety of domains, including communication, social, cognitive, and self-help skills; however, the most common regression is loss of language.[32][33]

There continues to be a debate over the differential outcomes based on these two developmental courses. Some studies suggest that regression is associated with poorer outcomes and others report no differences between those with early gradual onset and those who experience a regression period.[34] While there is conflicting evidence surrounding language outcomes in ASD, some studies have shown that cognitive and language abilities at age 2½ may help predict language proficiency and production after age 5.[35] Overall, the literature stresses the importance of early intervention in achieving positive longitudinal outcomes.[36]

### Social skills

Social skills present the most challenges for individuals with ASD. This leads to problems with friendships, romantic relationships, daily living, and vocational success.[37] Marriages are less common for those with ASD. Many of these challenges are linked to their atypical patterns of behavior and communication. It is common for children and adults with autism to struggle with social interactions because they are unable to relate to their peers.[38] All of these issues stem from cognitive impairments. Difficulties in this thought process is called "theory of the mind" or mind blindness which translates that the mind has difficulty with thought process as well as being aware of what is going on around them.[39] Theory of mind is closely related to the pragmatic difficulties children with autism experience.[40]

### Communication skills

Communication deficits are generally characterized by impairments regarding joint attention and social reciprocity, challenges with verbal language cues, and poor nonverbal communication skills [41] such as lack of eye contact and meaningful gestures and facial expressions.[42] Language behaviors typically seen in children with autism may include repetitive or rigid language, specific interests in conversation, and atypical language development.[42] ASD is a complex pragmatic language disorder which influences communication skills significantly.[43] Many children with ASD develop language skills at an uneven pace where they easily acquire some aspects of communication, while never fully developing other aspects.[42] In some cases, children remain completely nonverbal throughout their lives, although the accompanying levels of literacy and nonverbal communication skills vary.

They may not pick up on body language or may ignore cues such as eye contact and facial expressions if they provide more information than the person can process at that time. Similarly, they have trouble recognizing subtle expressions of emotion and identifying what various emotions mean for the conversation. They struggle with understanding the context and subtext of conversational or printed situations, and have trouble forming resulting conclusions about the content. This also results in a lack of social awareness and atypical language expression.[44]

It is also common for individuals with ASD to communicate strong interest in a specific topic, speaking in lesson-like monologues about their passion instead of enabling reciprocal communication with whomever they are speaking to.[42] What looks like self-involvement or indifference toward others stems from a struggle to realize or remember that other people have their own personalities, perspectives, and interests.[44] Language expression by those on the autism spectrum is often characterized by repetitive and rigid language. Often children with ASD repeat certain words, numbers, or phrases during an interaction, words unrelated to the topic of conversation. They can also exhibit a condition called echolalia in which they respond to a question by repeating the inquiry instead of answering.[42] However, this repetition can be a form of meaningful communication, a way that individuals with ASD try to express a lack of understanding or knowledge regarding the answer to the question.[45]

Not only do autistic children display difficulties with verbal language, they exhibit nonverbal behavior signals during communication. These nonverbal behavior signals are called paralinguistic features of communication. They are additions to the words being expressed that help determine the persons feelings or thoughts on a topic. While they might be telling you they are angry about something, they also might be gesturing by throwing their hands in the air to help express their anger. These signals include bodily contact, proximity, posture, head nods, and looking. There are many common bodily contact signals that people with autism display, but the most common are greetings and goodbyes. These can include the waving of hands to signal hello or goodbye. Individuals with ASD tend to stand closer or be closer to you when you are speaking. What is important to note for a person with ASD is that if they change their proximity towards you during a conversation, they are trying to end the discussion or are trying to change the discussion topic. The posture of an ASD person can determine the emotional state that they are in. If they are hunched over, one might be able to determine that they are upset or stressed about something occurring in their life. Head nods express the connection with speech. If a person nods their head once or twice they are comprehending what you say and understanding the topic at hand and what is being stated about it. If they nod more than once it is possible that the person with autism would like to say something and add to the conversation. While looking at another person while they speak might be an understood guideline for those without ASD, those with ASD may not have this. The might look away during a conversation and spend most time with an eye gaze not on the other communication partner. People with autism can be different in their nonverbal communication signals depending on the type of autism spectrum disorder they have.[46]

# Causes

While specific causes of autism spectrum disorders have yet to be found, many risk factors identified in the research literature may contribute to their development. These risk factors include genetics, prenatal and perinatal factors, neuroanatomical abnormalities, and environmental factors. It is possible to identify general risk factors, but much more difficult to pinpoint specific factors. In the current state of knowledge, prediction can only be of a global nature and therefore requires the use of general markers.[47]

### Genetic risk factors

As of 2018, understanding of genetic risk factors had shifted from a focus on a few alleles, to an understanding that genetic involvement in ASD is probably diffuse, depending on a large number of variants, some of which are common and have a small effect, and some of which are rare and have a large effect. The most common gene disrupted with large effect rare variants appeared to be CHD8, but less than 0.5% of people with ASD have such a mutation. Some ASD is associated with clearly genetic conditions, like fragile X syndrome; however only around 2% of people with ASD have fragile X.[48]

As of 2018, it appeared that somewhere between 74% and 93% of ASD risk is heritable and that after an older child is diagnosed with ASD, 7–20% of subsequent children are likely to be as well.[48] If parents have a child with ASD they have a 2% to 8% chance of having a second child with ASD. If the child with ASD is an identical twin the other will be affected 36 to 95 percent of the time. If they are fraternal twins the other will only be effected up to 31 percent of the time.[49]

### Prenatal and perinatal risk factors

Several prenatal and perinatal complications have been reported as possible risk factors for autism. These risk factors include maternal gestational diabetes, maternal and paternal age over 30, bleeding after first trimester, use of prescription medication (e.g. valproate) during pregnancy, and meconium in the amniotic fluid. While research is not conclusive on the relation of these factors to autism, each of these factors has been identified more frequently in children with autism compared to their non-autistic siblings and other typically developing youth.[50] While it is unclear if any single factors during the prenatal phase affect the risk of autism,[51] complications during pregnancy may be a risk.[51]

Low vitamin D levels in early development has been hypothesized as a risk factor for autism.[52]

### Vaccine controversy

Perhaps the most controversial claim regarding autism etiology was the "vaccine controversy".[53] This conjecture, arising from a case of scientific misconduct,[54] suggested that autism results from brain damage caused either by (1) the measles, mumps, rubella (MMR) vaccine itself, or by (2) thimerosal, a vaccine preservative.[55] No convincing scientific evidence supports these claims, and further evidence continues to refute them, including the observation that the rate of autism continues to climb despite elimination of thimerosal from routine childhood vaccines.[56] A 2014 meta-analysis examined ten major studies on autism and vaccines involving 1.25 million children worldwide; it concluded that neither the MMR vaccine, which has never contained thimerosal,[57] nor the vaccine components thimerosal or mercury, lead to the development of ASDs.[58]

# RESOURCES AND WEBSITES

ADOPTION and DONOR CONCEPTION FACTBOOK, THE
Available on Amazon

ADOPTIVE PARENTS FOR OPEN RECORDS & AGAINST ADOPTION
Facebook.com/Anti-AdoptionAdopters

CHILD WELFARE INFORMATION GATEWAY-
ADOPTION STATISTICS
(Federal Government website)
https://www.childwelfare.gov/topics/systemwide/statistics/adoption/

CONCERNED UNITED BIRTHPARENTS (CUB)
CUBirthparents.org

EMERGENCY, LIFE OR DEATH SEARCH
(Volunteers available sporadically) - ties-search.org
email: TIES@absnw.com

INNOCENCE NETWORK- BY STATE
InnocenceNetwork.org/members

INTERNATIONAL SOUNDEX REUNION REGISTRY (ISRR) - (Free)
isrr.org/Register.html

NATIONAL CENTER FOR MISSING & EXPLOITED CHILDREN
missingkids.com

PRISONER LOCATOR, BY STATE (Free)
ancestorhunt.com/prisonsearch

PRISONER LOCATOR, CALIFORNIA (Free)
inmatelocator.cdcr.cagov

PRISONER RESOURCES DIRECTORY (Free)
loricarangelo.com/prisoners/prisoners.html

MILITARY SEARCH
searchmil.com

PRIVATE INVESTIGATION NETWORK - P.I. MALL
pimall.com/

THE ULTIMATE SEARCH BOOK
U.S. and World Editions
available on Amazon

SEARCHABLE ONLINE DIRECTORIES
WhitePages.com (partly free)
- AnyWho.com
- 411.com
- Freeality.com (Free & for Fee)
- PeopleSearch.com (Fees apply)
- Intelius.com (Fees apply)
- Facebook.com
- MySpace.com
- Classmates.com
(Fee for contact)
- reunions.com
- DOBSEARCH.com

STATE BIRTH INDEXES
Visit a local FAMILY HISTORY CENTER or subscribe to Ancestry.com

SOCIAL SECURITY DEATH INDEX
rootweb.com; ancestry.com/search

RANCH HANDS DATABASE
searches.rootsweb.com

WORLDWIDE PHONE BOOKS
PhoneBooksoftheWorld.com

# BIBLIOGRAPHY

Akafat, Roman, *"International Adoption Corruption" What You Must Know Before You Adopt a Child or Children,"* Amazon, 2015

Associated Press (AP), *"Dekalb Woman's Relatives Charged With Murder,"* Rome News-Tribune, GA, 6-16-99, p. 3-A

Augusta State Prison (various staff), telephone followup, 2005 and 2013

Austin, Linda Tollet, *"Babies For Sale: The Tennessee Children's Home,"* Greenwood Press, 1993.

Benet, Mary K., *"The Politics of Adoption,"* The Free Press, 1976

Bloom, Dr. Lee, *"Growing Up Behind Locked Doors,"* Rolling Stone Magazine, 1986.

Bowlby, John., *"Illegitimacy and Deprivation,"* World Health Organization, Maternal Care and Mental Health Monograph Series 4, 2nd ed., 115,149,152; and *"Child Mourning and It's Implications for Psychiatry,"* American Journal of Psychiatry, The Alfred Mayer Lecture, p.481-498, 1961.

Callahan, Patrick J., Phd, in-person and telephone interviews, 2006

Cain, Bianca, *"Names of Inmates Charged in Fatal Augusta State Medical Prison Released,"* Augusta Chronicle, 7-14-11

Cano, Sandra,*"Sandra Cano, Doe v. Bolton Plaintiff: 'Abortion Is Something I Don't Believe In,"* Huff Post Live (online video), Huffington Post, Dallas, GA, 12-15-03; *"Testimony of Sandra Cano,"* United States Senate Judiciary Committee, 6-23-05; and telephone interviews, 2005 through 2013.

Cadoret, Remi, *"Biologic Perspectives of Adoptee Adjustment,"*(Brodzinsky), Oxford Press University , 1990.

Carp, E. Wayne, *"Jean Paton and the Struggle to Reform American Adoption,"* University of Michigan Press, 2014.

Chesler, Phyillis, *"Sacred Bond,"* and *"Mothers On Trial,"* 1986

CNN News, *"More Than 2000 Wrongfully Convicted People Exonerated in 23 Years, Researchers Say,*5-31-12.

Coles, Gary, *"The Invisible Men of Adoption,"* BookPOD, 2011.

Colevecchio-Van Sickler, *"Man Shoots Girlfriend, Rapes Girl, Then Kills Self,"* St. Petersburg Times, 8-18-04

D'Arcy, Claudia Corrigan, *"National Council For Adoption: Mothers, Money Marketing and Madness,"* Musings of the Lame, 2017.

Diver, Alice, *"A Law of Blood Ties: The Right to Access Genetic Ancestry,"* Springer Verlag, 2013"

Domingues, Joel Lee, interview and correspondence with Lori Carangelo, 2005 through 2007

Donalds, Elizabeth S., "*Voices of Adoptees: Stories and Experiences Within the Schools,*" Dissertation, Antioch University-New England, 2012.

Fariris, Theresa Rodrigues, "*When Adoption Fails,*" Housekeeper Publishing, 2008.

Fessler, Ann, "*The Girls Who Went Away,*" Penguin Books, 2007; and "*A Girl Like Her,*" (motion picture), LEF Foundation, Moving Image Fund, 2012.

FindLaw, "*Domingues v. State,*" Georgia Supreme Court No. S03A1458, 12-17-03

Fisher, Nancy L, MD, MPH, "*Cultural and Ethnic Diversity: A Guide for Genetics Professionals,*" John Hopkins University Press, 1966.

Fletcher, Sybil Lash, "*Supreme Deception,*" Sentinel Productions. 2002

Fuss, Inez Hyde (aka "Jackie"), "*Born January 4, 1925, Died June 21 1996, Decatur, Georgia.*"

Death Data, http://deathdata.org/r/31899788/inez-h-fuss; and Dekalb County Vital   Records

Georgia Department of Corrections Inmate Search Website, *Joel Lee Domingues, Charles Fuss, Melissa Erives, Margaret Branch*

Goldstein, L.A. and Carol R., "*Beyond the Best Interests of the Child,*" Free Press, 1972

Goodman, Attorney Kathleen A. Cassidy, http://boernelegal.com/ and telephone interviews, 2007

Goodman, Peter S., "*Stealing Babies for Adoption,*" Washington Post Foreign Service, 3-12-06.

Griffith, Keith, "*The Right to Know Who You Are,*" Katherine Kimball Publishing, 1992.

Hallowell, Billy, "*Meet Mary Doe...*" The Blaze, http://theblaze.com, 1-25-13

Hayes, John, "*Theft By Adoption,*" Amazon Books, 7-14-08.

Hood, G., "*Adoption or Abduction?*" Dan Rather Reports, AXS TV, 2012

Huy, Dao, *letters,* Innocence Project, New York, 2-10-10

Inglis, K., "*Living Mistakes: Mothers Who Consented to Adoption,*" G.Allen & Unwin, 1984

Innocence Project, "*Facts and Figures,*" FalseConfessions.org

Jalsevac, John, '*Two Women Are Behind Legal Abortion in America; Now Both of Them Want It  Reversed,*" Lifestyle News, http://lifestylenews.com, 1-17-13

Joyce, Kathryn, "*The Child Catcher: Rescue, Trafficking and the New Gospel of Adoption,*" Public Affairs, 2013

Kirk, H. David, "*Shared Fate: The Theory of Adoption and Mental Health,*" The Free Press of Glencoe, 1994.

Kirschner, David, Phd, "*Adoption Forensics: The Connection Between Adoption and Murder,*" Crime Magazine, 2007; and "*The Adopted Child*

Syndrome: Considerations for Psychotherapy," Adelphi Society, 1978,
Martin, Kaye, "Augusta State Medical Prison Ranks High in Assaults," Augusta
Lahl, Jennifer, "Baby Market As Financial Market," Center for Bioethics and
        Cultrure, 2016.
Maynard, Ray, "First Roe, Now Doe," World Magazine, 3-9-97
Maxwell, Aimee, citing "lack of funds," Innocence Project of Georgia
National Council For Adoption (NCFA), reference to "culture of adoption,"
        NCFA website
Newman, Maria, "Daughter of Woman in Abortion Case Takes a Pro-Choice
        Stand," Los Angeles Times, 11-16-89
Parker, Allen E., "Affidavit of Sandra Cano, the 'Doe' of Doe v. Bolton," Donna
        Santa Maria, Plaintiff et al v, Christine Todd Whitman et al,
        Defendants, U.S. District Court of New Jersey.
Reagan, Michael, "On the Outside Looking In," Zebra, 1988.
Riben, Marsha, "Shedding Light on the Dark Side of Adoption," Harlo Press,
        1988
Sack, Kevin, "Former Sheriff Is Charged With Killing Political Rival," New York
        Times, 12-1-01; and NewYorkTimes.com, "Former Sheriff Guilty in
        Successor Killing," 7-11-02
Samuels, Elizabeth, "How Adoption in America Grew Secret," Washington Post,
        2001.
Sauceda, Sandra Race Cano Domingues, "Affidavit of Sandra Cano," "Sandra
        Cano, Former 'Doe' in Doe v. Bolton and President of Wonderfully Made
        Ministry," http://VoteYesForLife.com; and phone interviews,
        2005 through 2013
Sawyer, Josh, "Death By Adoption," Cicada Press, 2014.
Seattle Times, "Killer's Guilt Disputed," 6-21-99
Solinger, Rickie, "Pregnancy and Power: A History of Reproductive Politics in
        America," NYU Press United States District Court for Northern
        Georgia, "Sandra Cano, formerly known as Mary Doe, v. Arthur Bolton,
        Attorney General of Georgia," Civil Case # 13676
University of Michigan, National Registry of Exonerations, 2013 Report
Verrier, Nancy Newton, "Primal Wound: Understanding the Adopted Child,"
        Gateway Press, 2003.
WAG-TV News-Atlanta, "Augusta State Prison Guard Caught Smuggling in
        Narcotics."
Walker, Leslie: "A Sudden Fury: A True Story of Adoption and Murder,"
        St. Martin's Press, 1989
Walsh, Lauren, "Exclusive: Prison Guard Caught at Work with Drugs, Charged
        with Intent to Distribute," NBC-26 TV News 7-13-12; also Augusta
        Chronicle, and WAG-TV News-Atlanta, 7-13-12.
Weigel, Margaret and John Whitby, "False Confessions, New Data and

*Law Enforcement Interrogations: Research Findings,"*
JournalistsResource.org, 1-15-15

Wellisch, E., *"Children Without Genealogy – A Problem of Adoption,"* Mental
Health 13, 1952.

White, Gayle, *"Estate Dispute Led to Slayings Police Say,"* Atlanta Journal-
Constitution,
6-17-99; *"Roe v. Wade Just a Page in a Rocky Life,"* Atlanta Journal-
Constitution, 1-22-03, p.1A; and phone interviews with Gayle White

Wilson-Buterbaugh, Karen, *"The Baby Scoop Era: Unwed Mothers, Infant
Adoption and Forced Surrender,"* Amazon Books, 2017.

Wikipedia, *"Sydney Dorsey,"* https://en.wikipedia.org/wiki/Sidney_Dorsey

WND-Radio America, *"The Woman Who Started Legal Abortion,"* broadcast
and online video, 1-23-13

# INDEX

# PHOTOS and ILLUSTRATIONS LIST

## ABOUT THE AUTHOR

LORI CARANGELO's 1963 Hamden (Connecticut) High School yearbook predicted "a career in Child Welfare." But Lori instead devoted much of her life to *opposing* the corrupt Child Welfare System. Her national network of volunteers assisted thousands of adoptees, without charge, in obtaining information and contact with their biological families.

Born in 1945 to Italian-American parents in New Haven, Connecticut, she is retired from 25 years in administrative positions in Santa Barbara and Palm Desert, California, where she also authored over 600 published articles and 25 unique non-fiction books. Her "true crime" books endeavor to answer the question as to *"WHY* they did it, while *"BLOOD RELATVES"* and *"EYEWITNESS"* were undertaken to give voice and support to the wrongfully convicted.

Also by Lori Carangelo:

ADOPTED KILLERS
*430 Adoptees Who Killed – How and Why They Did It*

CHOSEN CHILDREN
*Children as Commodities in America's Failed
Foster Car, Adoption and Immigration Systems*

THE ULTIMATE SEARCH BOOK
*U.S. and Worldwide Editions*

THE ADOPTION AND DONOR CONCEPTION FACTBOOK
*The Only Comprehensive Source of U.S. & Global Data
on the Hidden Families of Foster Care, Adoption and Donor Conception*

SCHOOL SHOOTERS
*Why They Did It and America's War on Guns*

SERIAL KILLERS ON THE INTERSTATE -
*200 Highway Killers by State*

KONDRO
*The "Uncle Joe" Killer*

JAMES MUNRO – *And the Freeway Killers*

EYEWITNESS
*The Case of the Carefully Crafted Central Coast Rapist?*

8 BALL CAFÉ
*Adoption, Addiction and Redemption*

RAGE!
*How An Adoption Ignited A Fire*

ESPOSITO
*The First Mafioso*

www.ingramcontent.com/pod-product-compliance
Lightning Source LLC
Chambersburg PA
CBHW071557040426
42452CB00008B/1200